JESUS DEATH
WAS NOT
IN VAIN

KNOW WHO YOU ARE IN CHRIST

PATRICIA COLEMAN

Order this book online at www.trafford.com
or email orders@trafford.com

Most Trafford titles are also available at major online book retailers.

Printed in the United States of America.

ISBN: 978-1-4669-3994-3 (sc)
ISBN: 978-1-4669-3993-6 (e)

Trafford rev. 05/24/2012

www.trafford.com

North America & international
toll-free: 1 888 232 4444 (USA & Canada)
phone: 250 383 6864 ✦ fax: 812 355 4082

CONTENTS

CHAPTER 1   Know Who You Are in Christ 1

CHAPTER 2   The Word Is Life to Those
Who Find It 9

CHAPTER 3   There Is No Fear Here 15

CHAPTER 4   Beware of Letting Strife into Your Life 27

CHAPTER 5   Protect the Anointing 33

CHAPTER 6   The Angels Are Here to Serve You 38

CHAPTER 7   If God Be for You, Who Can Be
Against You? 42

CHAPTER 8   Enter God's Rest 49

CHAPTER 9   Become a Doer of the Word and Not
a Hearer Only 53

CHAPTER 10   How to Receive What Jesus Died for
You to Have 61

CHAPTER 11   God Has a People on the Earth
(Are You One of Them?) 69

CHAPTER 12   The Key to Keeping Your Faith Strong
in God 77

CHAPTER 1

KNOW WHO YOU ARE IN CHRIST

Isaiah 54:14 says, "In righteousness you shall be established; you shall be far from oppression, for you shall not fear; And from terror, for it shall not come near you." Do you know what it means to be established in righteousness? It means to be right with God—to be able to stand in the presence of a holy, awesome, almighty God without a sense of guilt or inferiority. Think about that! What must it be like to be established in righteousness? What must it be like to know without a shadow of a doubt that there is absolutely nothing wrong between you and God? No, sir, nothing. What must it be like for everything to be so right that every time you walk in the door, the Father says, "Yes, yes, yes," before you can even ask him for anything?

It is easy for us to believe things are that way between God and Jesus. But please realize this: you were given the righteousness of God through exactly the same miraculous occurrences that made him sin with your sin. Here is 2 Corinthians 5: 16-21:

> Wherefore henceforth know we no man after the flesh;
> yea, though we have known Christ after the flesh, yet now
> henceforth know we him no more. Therefore if any man be

in Christ, he is a new creature; old things are passed away; behold, all things are new. And all things are of God; who hath reconciled us to himself by Jesus Christ, and hath given to us the ministry of reconciliation; To wit, that God was in Christ, reconciling the world unto himself, not imputing their trespasses unto them; and hath committed unto us the word of reconciliation. Now then we are ambassadors for Christ, as though God did beseech you by us: we pray you in Christ's stead, be ye reconciled to God. For he hath made him to be sin for us, who knew no sin; that we might be made the righteousness of God in him.

We have the same entrance to our heavenly Father because of what Jesus did. I know that may be hard for some of us to understand, but we have to keep working on it. We have to keep thinking about it all the time; we have to keep meditating on it and developing a righteousness consciousness instead of a sin consciousness.

God's power will help you. (It is not willpower.) Your willpower is there to make the choice, but the power of God is what empowers you to stand for what you know God wants you to do. A person who is not born again does not have the power of God, because his spirit is dead and there is no life of God in him; willpower is all such a person has. First John 3:7-10 says,

Little children, let no one deceive you. He who practices righteousness is righteous, just as He is righteous. He who sins is of the devil, for the devil has sinned from the beginning. For this purpose the Son of God was manifested, that he might destroy the works of the devil. Whoever has been born of God does not sin, for His seed remains in him; and he cannot sin, because he has been born of God. In this the children of God and the children of the devil are manifest: Whoever does not practice righteousness is not of God, nor is he who does not love his brother.

We have authority to crucify the flesh. You have to talk to your flesh, because it wants to do what it wants to do. You have to tell your flesh, "You are not going to have your way. I am a child of God, and I am not going to do and practice the things that are displeasing to him. I am going to practice righteousness. I am the righteousness of God in Christ Jesus." Die for him. What will happen as you do that? You will not be afraid to do exploits in Jesus's name. You will not be afraid to act like him. You will not be afraid boldly to claim what is yours in Jesus Christ. You will not be afraid to lay hands on the sick, believing they will recover. You will not be afraid to believe God for your healing or for the finances you need. So become skillful in the word of righteousness. Receive that you have been made the righteousness of God in Christ. Receive that you are established in righteousness. Stand and be what God intended you to be without any sense of guilt or inferiority and live in victory every day. It is your God-given right as a child of God.

Second Corinthians 5 says, "Therefore if any man be in Christ, he is a new creation; old things have passed away; behold, all things have become new . . . For He made Him who knew no sin to be sin for us, that we might become the righteousness of God in him"(verses 17 and 21). The devil is afraid that Christians are going to find out just who they are in Christ and the power and authority Christ has given them, because when they do, the devil's days in their lives will be numbered. So naturally the devil tries to keep you ignorant of God's will for you. Until you know who you are and the authority you have in Jesus's name, you are not being all that God wants you to be. He needs you; you are his hands and feet here on the earth. We are the ones God will use to put the devil in his proper place, which is under our feet. God sent his only son, Jesus, to die for us not only to forgive our sins but also to redeem us back from under the devil's control. To be redeemed means to be returned to the original state. The second Adam has returned us to the original authority that man had under God before the first Adam sinned.

Galatians 3:10: "For as many as are under the works of the law are under the curse; for it is written, "Cursed is every one that continueth not in all the things which are written in the book of the law to do

3

them." Here is the problem! So many of God's children are still under the curse. That verse says, "For as many as are under the works of the law are under the curse." You are not saved by doing things for God; you are saved by God's grace. It is a gift from God so that no one can boast (Ephesians 2:8).

This is how the devil controls God's people: he gets them to think that they can earn their way to heaven by doing some great things for God, when in actuality you are saved by grace, lest any man should boast (praise God). Did you get that? It is only by your faith in God's son that you are saved. John 3:16 says, "For God so loved the world, that he gave his only begotten son, that whosoever believeth in him should not perish, but have everlasting life."

When you really get a revelation of who you are in Christ and the power and authority that Christ has given you, the devil's days are over in your life. That is how he controls us—by ignorance. Not knowing who you are means still living under the curse. The Bible says in Colossians 1:13 that the Father has delivered and drawn us to himself out of the control and dominion of darkness and has transferred us into the kingdom of the son of his love. Do you know what that is saying? At one time, before Jesus came, we were under the devil's control after Adam and Eve sinned in the garden, but now God has delivered and drawn us to himself out of the control of the devil (read that scripture again). If that does not make you shout, I do not know what will. We have been transferred out of darkness into the kingdom of the son of his love. God loves us so much, he gave his son so we could live. (If that is not love, I do not know what is.)

It is time for the body of Christ to quit playing church. God did not give his son to die for us just to have something to do. Adam sold out to the devil, and God made a way for us. Let's read Colossians 1:13 again: "Who hath delivered us from the power of darkness, and hath translated us into the kingdom of his dear Son." This scripture is saying a lot. When Adam sinned, he took everything. In the beginning, God gave Adam dominion over everything, but when he sinned, he lost it; he was no longer in the kingdom of God's dear son; he was transferred into the devil's kingdom, and keep in mind that the devil's kingdom is under the curse. But when Jesus came and we accepted him as our lord, we were no longer under the curse; we were transferred into the kingdom of God's dear son, where the blessings are. God said in Deuteronomy 30:19-20, "I call heaven and earth to record this day against you, that I have set before you life and death, blessings and cursing: therefore choose life, that both thou and thy seed may live: That thou mayest love the Lord thy God, and that thou mayest obey his voice, and that thou mayest cleave unto him: for he is thy life, and the length of thy days: that thou mayest dwell in the land which the lord sware unto thy fathers, to Abraham, to Isaac, and to Jacob, to give them."

We must become Kingdom of God-minded. When Jesus was here on the earth, he spoke often about his Father's kingdom. He told Pontius Pilate, "My kingdom is not of this world: if my kingdom were of this world, then would my servants fight, that I should not be delivered to the Jews: but now is my kingdom not from hence" (John 18:36). We must have the same attitude that Jesus had: we must become Kingdom of God-minded. If we do not, we will get too comfortable here on this earth just meeting our needs and our families' needs. As believers, we need to become aware that although we are in the world, we do not belong to its natural order. We are citizens of heaven (praise God). We are privileged to live in the kingdom right now. Many would probably not believe what I just said, because religion has taught people that they will not reach God's kingdom until they die and go to heaven, but let's read Colossians 1:13 again: the Father "hath delivered us from the power of darkness, and hath translated us into the kingdom of his dear Son." So according to this scripture, we have been transferred into the kingdom of God's son. So when we accept Jesus as our personal savior, we are transferred right then before we go to heaven. Is that great or what? So we do not have to wait to go to heaven to receive life. Look at John 10:10. "The thief [the devil] cometh not, but for to steal, and to kill, and to destroy: I [Jesus] am come that they might have life, and that they might have it more abundantly."

There is a devil out there trying to keep you in ignorance and fear so you will not go after what Jesus has already died for you to have. When Jesus died he took your sins, but he took a lot more than that. Look at 1 Peter 2:24. "Who his own self bare our sins in his own body on the tree, that we, being dead to sins, should live unto righteousness; by whose stripes ye were healed." He also took our sicknesses and diseases. Second Corinthians 8:9 says, "For ye know the grace of our Lord Jesus Christ, that, though he was rich, yet for your sakes he became poor, that ye through his poverty might be rich." Jesus also took your poverty so you could be rich. No wonder the devil wants to keep you ignorant of what the word says you are in Christ! Hosea 4:6 says, "My people are destroyed for lack of knowledge: because thou hast rejected knowledge, I will also reject thee, that thou shalt be no priest to me: seeing thou hast forgotten the law of thy God, I will also forget thy children." Not only is God saying that people are destroyed for a lack of knowledge, but he goes on to say that because they have rejected knowledge, he will reject them. Did you know that sometimes people just do not want to know things concerning God? The more they know, the more responsible they are to God. I do not know about you, but I refuse to live in ignorance of God's word. I refuse to let the devil steal another thing from me. We do not have to be ignorant of the devil's devices. Learn who you are in Christ Jesus and put the devil where he belongs—under your feet. If you will stay with God's word and stay on that word, you can become what God meant you to become: a blood-covenant child of the almighty God who possesses the righteousness of God and has authority over all the works of the devil. You can take your rightful place here on earth, take your dominion and power back, and put the devil where he belongs—under your feet.

Jesus died for you, and he stripped the devil of all the power that Adam gave him when he sinned. And Jesus gave that power back to you and me. John 1:11-13 says, "He came unto his own, and his own received him not. But as many as received him, to them gave he power to become the sons of God, even to them that believe on his name: Which were born, not of blood, nor of the will of the flesh; nor of the will of man, but of God."

The devil definitely does not want you to find out who you are in Christ, because when you do, he knows it will be over for him. No longer will he be able to control you through ignorance.

Romans 12:1-2 says, "I beseech you therefore, brethren, by the mercies of God, that ye present your bodies a loving sacrifice, holy, acceptable unto God, which is your reasonable service. And be not conformed to this world: but be ye transformed by the renewing of your mind, that ye may prove what is that good, and acceptable, and perfect, will of God." In verse 2 of Romans 12, we are told not to be conformed to this world but to be transformed by the renewing of our minds. So how do we do that? In order to get God's thoughts, we must read his word. I will give you a perfect example of what I am saying here: if the doctors said you had an incurable disease and you were going to die in a few months, would you accept the doctor's word, or would you believe what God says in I Peter 2:24, that Jesus "his own self bare our sins in his own body on the tree, that we, being dead to sins, should live unto righteousness; by whose stripes ye were healed." This is how we get our minds renewed.

We find out in the word of God what God says about things, and we put our faith in that. I can tell you from experience that once you renew your mind to conform to what God says, this Christian walk gets easier. As long as we are in this physical body, we are going to have to deal with our flesh. I remember years ago when I was dealing with fear of displeasing God. I love God so much that I was afraid I would displease him. So I prayed, and God spoke these verses to my heart, and after that I never thought that way again:

> There is therefore now no condemnation to them which are in Christ Jesus, who walk not after the flesh, but after the Spirit. For the law of the Spirit of life in Christ Jesus hath made me free from the law of sin and death. For what the law could not do, in that it was weak through the flesh, God sending his own Son in the likeness of sinful flesh, and for sin, condemned sin in the flesh: That the righteousness of the law might be fulfilled in us, who walk not after the flesh, but after the Spirit. (Romans 8:1-4)

After God spoke those words to my heart, I never questioned again whether I would displease him. He was letting me know that as long as I walked in the spirit, there would be no problems. But sad to say, this is a big problem in the body of Christ. As long as we are led by our

7

flesh, feelings, desires, and so on, we will never please God. The more we read the word of God, the more we will think like God. Just to show you how important it is to have the mind of Christ, let's read Romans 8:6-8: "For to be carnally minded is death; but to be spiritually minded is life and peace. Because the carnal mind is enmity against God: for it is not subject to the law of God, neither indeed can be. So then they that are in the flesh cannot please God." I do not know about you, but I never want to be in a position where I do not please God. So when God says to have our minds renewed so that we can prove what the perfect will of God is, it is for our advantage. Actually, everything God tells us to do is for our advantage. He loves us.

There are four things we must do to renew our minds:

1. read the word of God,
2. go to a church where the word is preached,
3. meditate on the word and think deeply about it, and
4. listen to tapes and CDs that teach the word.

CHAPTER 2

THE WORD IS LIFE
TO THOSE WHO FIND IT

The reading of God's word is so important. Let's look at Joshua 1:8. "This book of the law shall not depart out of thy mouth; but thou shalt meditate therein day and night, that thou mayest observe to do according to all that is written therein: for then thou shalt make thy way prosperous, and then thou shalt have good success." Do you think the devil wants you to have good success? Remember John 10:10: the devil comes to kill, steal, and destroy. I want to encourage you to fill yourself with the word of God so there is not room in your heart for unbelief, doubt, or fear. Saturate your heart until the word naturally begins to flow out of your mouth. Let it completely take over and renew you mind. Remember that Romans 12:2 says, "And be not conformed to this world: but be ye transformed by the renewing of your mind, that ye may prove what is that good, and acceptable, and perfect, will of God." God's word is his will. Did you know that your future is determined by you? Look at Matthew 12:34-35: "Out of the abundance of the heart the mouth speaketh. A good man out of the good treasure of the heart bringeth forth good things: and an evil man out of the evil treasure bringeth forth evil things." Jesus said that what is in your heart is what comes forth, so get the word in your heart. The more you deposit God's word in your heart, the better things are, because that is where you will draw from to change the circumstances in your life. Your future is really stored up in your heart, and it's up to you whether it will be a bright future or a dark future.

Jesus said in John 15:7, "If ye abide in me, and my words abide in you, ye shall ask what ye will, and it shall be done unto you." God's words are living forces and are very powerful. If you allow them to take residence in you, they will produce holiness in your life. To be holy is to be separated for God's use. If you allow your choices to be bathed in the authority of God's word, these choices will separate you from the destructive bent of this natural world and take you into the blessings of the supernatural realm. We make decisions that can either damage or enrich lives all around us. That is why it is important to go to the word and get God's thoughts on the matter. We can save ourselves so much heartache and pain by spending quality time in God's word and in his presence. If we will just let him, God will help us with every choice we make. So start getting the word into your heart now. Let the force of it and the enormity of it direct your choices, big and small. Let God begin to lift you up to his way of thinking. God's word will show you how to live a victorious life even in a dark world. When you walk according to God's word and abide in that word, it will shine light on your path. The apostle Peter talks about the light of the word of God. He says to pay close attention to it like you would a lamp shining in a dark place. If you focus your attention on the word of God, you can fight the good fight of faith and win even when negative circumstances are all around you. Keep your eyes on Jesus, and you will have light. It will bring you through to victory every time (praise God). You can have faith strong enough to change the circumstances in your life. You can live in victory instead of defeat. But you will only do it by continually spending time in God's word.

The second verse of 1 Peter 2 says, "Desire the sincere milk of the word, that ye may grow thereby." I looked up the word *desire*. It means "to crave, to long for, or to ask for." When we meditate on the word, we give our spirit something to grow on. When you bring the spirit in control over your mind and your body, you will still have to fight the fight of faith to keep them in line. But as long as you are walking in the spirit, you will succeed every time. The word is spiritual food; the more of it you put in your heart, the stronger your spirit becomes. If you will continually feed on the word, eventually your spirit will be so dominant that it can overcome your flesh every time. The opposite is also true: if you spend your time feeding on soap operas, romance novels, and such, your flesh will grow stronger and your spirit will weaken. You may still have the inner desire to be loving and kind, but the flesh will bully you into acting like the devil. John 8:31-32 says, "Then said Jesus to those Jews which believed on him, If ye continue in my word, then are ye my disciples indeed; And ye shall know the truth, and the truth shall make you free." So by continuing to study God's word, we prove that we are his disciples. He said that the truth of God's word will make us free. Continuing in the word will help the fruit of the spirit to flow in your life and make you free from the bondage of the flesh. In reality, we have already won, but the enemy of your soul, the devil, does not want you to know that truth. The devil has no authority over a born-again child of God. He has to intimidate you and make you think that he has authority. But just remember Jesus stripped the devil of all the authority he had.

Hosea said, "My people are destroyed for a lack of knowledge." Having knowledge of the word of God can mean life or death to an individual. I will give you an example. Say you have not eaten in days and are starving to death and someone buys food for you but neglects to tell you about it. If you do not know that they bought you the food, it will not help you; you will starve to death. It is the same way with spiritual food (God's word). If you have a Bible and never read what it says, it cannot help you. Just as we need physical food to stay alive, spiritual food is just as important. Jesus said in Matthew 4:4, "Man shall not live by bread alone, but by every word that proceedeth out of the mouth of God." The more of the word you have in your heart—not just in your head knowledge—the better equipped you are to handle whatever problems you face. In my own life, before I really knew that Jesus had taken my sickness and pain and that I did not have to be sick, I was sick a lot. I accepted every cold or whatever that came along. The key word is *accepted.* The Bible says that every sickness and every disease is under the curse, and Galatians 3:13 says I have been redeemed from the curse of the law, so I have been redeemed from every sickness and disease there is. Of course, I cannot stop the symptoms, but I sure do not have to accept them. I take my stand any time any kind of sickness tries to invade my body. I let the devil know that Jesus has redeemed me from the curse of sickness and that by the stripes of Jesus I am healed. I stand on the word of God. Sometimes the symptoms leave immediately, and other times they linger, but whatever happens, I never accept sickness in my body. I take my medicine, which is God's word, and I stand on that word. After a while, my body lines up with the words I am saying, and the symptoms leave. On the other hand, if you start confessing that you are sick, then that is what you will experience. We experience what we say, so be careful of the words you speak. When you do your part by believing, speaking, and acting based on a heart full of faith, God's word will come to pass. No circumstance on earth and no demon in hell can stop it.

Psalm 119:105 talks more about the value of knowing God's word: "Thy word is a lamp unto my feet, and a light unto my path." When you think about a lamp, you think of the light that comes from that lamp to light your way so you can know where you are going. The word of God, of course, is that lamp, and the more you know, the better equipped you are to walk God's way. You will never find yourself in a situation in which you exercise faith in God's word and God fails to keep his word. Jeremiah 1:12 says that God is "active and alert, watching over his word to perform it" (AMP). The less we know about God's word, the more power it gives the devil. I like how the psalmist brings that out in Psalm 119:11-12: "Thy word I have hid in mine heart, that I might not sin against thee. Blessed art thou, O Lord: teach me thy statutes." It is to our advantage to study the word of God. It is very difficult to do something if you do not know what it is you are supposed to do. By reading the word and by spending time in prayer and continual fellowship with the Father, you can stay on the path to everlasting life, and as the word says in John 8:32, "ye shall know the truth, and the truth shall make you free."

God has promised many blessings for his people, and we will receive everything that he has for us if we believe and appropriate that which belongs to us. Numbers 23:19 says, "God is not a man, that he should lie; neither the son of man, that he should repent: hath he said, and shall he not do it? or hath he spoken, and shall he not make it good?" So the problem is not with God but with us. Although God has promised us many things in his word, we are not going to receive those things just because God said we would; there is a condition. Deuteronomy 30:19-20 says, "I call heaven and earth to record this day against you, that I have set before you life and death, blessing and cursing: therefore choose life, that both thou and thy seed may live: That thou mayest love the LORD thy God, and that thou mayest obey his voice, and that thou mayest cleave unto him: for he is thy life, and the length of thy days: that thou mayest dwell in the land which the Lord sware unto thy fathers, to Abraham, to Isaac, and to Jacob, to give them." The scripture says that God sets blesses and curses, and we must choose. The choice concerns more than just us. It also concerns our loved ones and neighbors. What much of the body of Christ does not understand is that how we live our lives affects how much of God's blessing we receive. There is much division and strife in the body of Christ, and it should not be that way. When Jesus was with his disciples at the Last Supper, he gave them a new commandment. John 13: 34-35 says, "A new commandment I give unto you, That ye love one another; as I have loved you, that ye also love one another. By this shall all men know that ye are my disciples, if ye have love one to another." Too many Christians talk about how much they love God but have no love for their brothers and sisters. And they do not connect that with why God is not blessing them as he said he would. And believe me, he waits to bless us more than we want to be blessed, but his hands are tied, so to speak. God cannot break his laws. In Matthew 5:44-48, Jesus said,

> But I say unto you, Love your enemies, bless them that curse you, do good to them that hate you, and pray for them which despitefully use you, and persecute you; That ye may be the children of your Father which is in heaven: for he maketh

his sun to rise on the evil and on the good, and sendeth rain on the just and on the unjust. For if ye love them which love you, what reward have ye? do not even the publicans the same? And if ye salute your brethren only, what do ye more than others? do not even the publicans so? Be ye therefore perfect, even as your Father which is in heaven is perfect.

So in order to be blessed by God, we must be obedient and do what he says to do in his word. I do not know about you, but if I see in God's word something that I should or should not be doing, I start or stop doing it immediately so I can live up to what the word of God says I should be doing. I am very determined that I will have God's blessings in my life. I cannot live without them. Just because things are a little slow in coming or do not manifest as quickly as we anticipate does not mean that God's promises are not true, because they are. We must have strong faith in what God has promised, but we also need patience. Hebrews 10:35-36 says, "Cast not away therefore your confidence, which hath great recompence of reward. For ye have need of patience, that, after ye have done the will of God, ye might receive the promise." So everything God has promised shall come to pass; we just need to be patient and trust God that what he has promised will come to pass in his timing, not ours.

CHAPTER 3

THERE IS NO FEAR HERE

Fear is the only weapon that the devil has, but it has been working well for him. That is why it is so important that the born-again children of God realize just who we are in Christ and what Jesus has done for us. Ephesians 6:10-11 says, "Finally, my brethren, be strong in the Lord, and in the power of his might. Put on the whole amour of God, that ye may be able to stand against the wiles of the devil." I looked up *wiles,* and it means "trickery or magic."

The devil has no authority. He tricks people into believing that he has power. One of the things he uses most is fear. That is why it is so important that we know what the word says. In 2 Timothy 1:7, the apostle Paul writes, "For God hath not given us the spirit of fear; but of power, and of love, and of a sound mind." When the devil tempted Jesus in Matthew chapter 4, Jesus always came back with the word, and we have to do the same.

Revelation 12:11 says, "And they overcame him [the devil] by the blood of the Lamb, and by the word of their testimony; and they loved not their lives unto the death." Fear is faith in reverse. When you fear, you will not receive anything from God. Luke 12:32 says, "Fear not, little flock; for it is your Father's good pleasure to give you the Kingdom." If you just stay with God and stay in his word, you can stop the fear. Did you know that obeying the word is an act of courage? When you obey the word and believe God in a situation, you are swimming upstream; you are going against the current of the world. A lot of people mentally assent. They say, "I believe that God can heal me," but when they get sick they pray and the pain does not go away. Then they say, "Well, I guess God did not heal me." But if you believe the word that says by the stripes of Jesus we are healed, you will not let the symptoms keep you from believing God even if there is pain. We do not deny the pain in our bodies; we just deny its right to stay in our bodies. We keep saying that by the stripes of Jesus we were healed until our bodies line up with the word. When you start believing the promises of God and start walking toward your victory over sickness or sin, the devil will tell you that you are just a natural person, but he is a lair. You have been born again. Jesus is living in you. You are the righteousness of God, an ambassador of Christ. The devil will tell you that you cannot trust the supernatural power of God to pull you through, but do not believe him. All he can do is talk and try to get you to fear. Remember that he has no power. He has to trick you into believing that he has power; that is the only way he can harm you—with your consent. That is why you need to learn to think with the mind of Christ. You need to live with your thoughts on the things of God instead of the things of this world. God wants us to rest in his power. He wants us to know him so well and trust him so much that when the devil tries to threaten us, we can just laugh at him. In my own life, before I really got it, the devil used to intimidate me, but now I just laugh at him. Jesus said the prince of this world is coming, but he has no hold on you (John 12:31). You and I need to come to a place in this world where we trust God with every detail of our lives. Start practicing today, believe his word, speak it to your problems, and watch faith rise. It works for me. I know it can work for you as well.

Psalm 141:3 says, "Set a watch, O Lord, before my mouth; keep the door of my lips." That scripture is talking about how we have to be careful of the things we say. Did you know that the devil cannot do anything to you unless you give him a place in your life—for example, by speaking words of doubt and unbelief? But if you speak words of faith, the devil cannot do anything with that. As I said before, if you are a born-again child of God, the devil has no authority over you unless you let him have that authority. The devil is out to steal the words of God out of your heart. That is the only way he can get a foothold in your life, so only speak words of faith, even under pressure (especially under pressure, no matter what the devil is saying to you in your thoughts. It does not matter what people around you are saying. Just keep agreeing with the word of God. Keep saying what God says. It is not easy sometimes, but believe me, it is worth it. When things look bad, do not speak negatively. If you are believing God for money and it seems like instead of the money coming in things are getting worse, just keep your eyes off of the lack of money and put them on God. Double up on your confession and start expecting God to move in your finances, and he will. (I know this from experience.) The devil's job is to make you look at the problems, but if you take your focus away from the problems and start focusing on Jesus, the problem solver, luck will be a things of the past. The devil knows what God can and will do in our lives, and he is trying desperately to stop us from trusting God to meet our needs. Refuse to allow the devil to intimidate you with threats. He can only do what we say. He does not have any authority over us unless we give it to him.

In Genesis 1:26-28, we read, "And God said, Let us make man in our image, after our likeness: and let them have dominion over the fish of the sea, and over the fowl of the air, and over the cattle, and over all the earth, and over every creeping thing that creepeth upon the earth . . . And God blessed them, and God said unto them, Be fruitful, and multiply, and replenish the earth, and subdue it: and have dominion over the fish of the sea, and over the fowl of the air, and over every living thing that moveth upon the earth."

I looked up the word *dominion* from verse 28, and it means "to have power to rule or govern a territory." So in this scripture, Adam and Eve were given the power to rule the earth. And just as God gave them authority to rule the earth, he has given us authority over the earth as well. He told his disciples in Acts 1:8 that they would receive power from the Holy Spirit to witness to all the earth.

God has given us authority or dominion over our households and families, but if we do not exercise that authority, the devil will come in and take over our lives just as he did with Adam and Eve, and you know what happened there. Because they disobeyed God and ate from the tree, they were put out of the garden. In 1 Peter 5:8, it says, "Be sober, be vigilant; because your adversary the devil, as a roaring lion, walketh about, seeking whom he may devour." It does not say the devil *is* a lion; he only acts like one, so he can not devour you unless you let him. Remember, Jesus stripped Satan of all his powers, so he does not have any power, but he wants you to think that he does. That is the way he gets back into the born-again believer's life. Do not let him. When we were born again, the Bible says we were delivered out of the control and dominion of darkness into the kingdom of God's son (Colossians 1:13). He has delivered us from the power of darkness and transferred us into the kingdom of his love.

Since we have been delivered out of the devil's kingdom, the devil no longer has any right of lordship over us. We have received salvation. But salvation includes a lot more than just going to heaven when we die. It includes all the blessings of God: peace, healing, prosperity, and every provision for every area of our lives. It all belongs to us the moment we make Jesus the lord of our lives.

But of course the devil does not want you to enjoy the blessings of God. He does not want you to walk in divine health or to be happy and prosperous, because if you do, other people will notice and want what you have. They will give their hearts to the lord because of the goodness of God they see in your life.

So the devil's job is to keep you sad, depressed, and living a defeated life. John 10:10, one of my favorite scriptures, says that the devil comes to steal and to kill, but Jesus came that we may have life and have it more abundantly.

The devil has no authority over your life anymore. He has to trick you or deceive you into opening the door of your life to him. James 4:7 says, "Submit yourselves therefore to God. Resist the devil, and he will flee from you." Verse 8 goes on the say, and this is very important, "Draw nigh to God, and he will draw nigh to you. Cleanse your hands, ye sinners, and purge your hearts, ye double minded." James says to resist the devil, so when the devil speaks words to you that are contrary to God's word, do not listen to him.

Rebuke him in Jesus's name and put your mind back to the word of God and say out loud the scriptures that apply to your situation.

Joshua 1:8 says, "This Book of the Law shall not depart from your mouth, but you shall meditate in it day and night, that you may observe to do according to all that is written in it. For then you will make your way prosperous, and then you will have good success." We must be determined to spend time in God's word every day. I know that may sound easy, but this is where many believers miss it. The devil could not stop you from receiving Jesus into your life, so now he will try to stop you from reading God's word. Remember that he has no authority over you any longer, so he has to get you to work for him by trying to pull you away from what God says. That is the only way he can get an opening in your life; that is his only hope. So we must speak faith only. Agree only with what the word says. The devil cannot do anything to you if you do not open the door to him with your words. The devil has no authority over you. He only wants you to think he has. He cannot rob you unless you authorize that robbery yourself. He comes to your words, so be careful what you say. Only speak God's word. Do not give the devil a foothold into your life. The devil is not the only enemy of your soul. You also have the flesh to conquer. Of course, the flesh is under subjection to God's will. It says in 1 Peter 4:1-2, "Therefore, since Christ suffered for us in the flesh, arm yourselves also with the same mind, for he who has suffered in the flesh has ceased from sin, that he no longer should live the rest of his time in the flesh for the lusts of men, but for the will of God." I especially like the second verse: "that he no longer should live the rest of his time in the flesh." For the lusts of man but for the will of God. So we must crucify the flesh. We must no longer live in this world to do what the flesh feels like it wants to do. If you will develop your Spirit and put him in charge of your body instead of being dominated by the flesh, eventually you will train your body to work with your Spirit instead of against it. Galatians 5:16-17 Says, so if you walk in the Spirit you cannot please the flesh. So make it a practice to read God's word daily and get your minds renewed to

God's way of thinking. At Hebrews 4:12 It says that the word of God is quick, and powerful, and sharper than any twoedged sword, piercing even to the dividing asunder of soul and spirit, and of the joints and marrow, and is a discerner of the thoughts and intents of the heart.

That means that if you believe God for something that is based on his word, you can rest assured that God is faithful to keep his word. He will not fail you. His word is alive, and it works for you every time you speak it and act on it in faith. So be determined to have everything that Jesus died for you to have. Be determined that you will have divine health, prosperity, peace, joy, and every other blessing that Jesus died for you to have. Did you know that God wants you to live a good life? Jesus died for us to have it all, but the devil tries to steal our blessings from us. (But saints do not let him.) Just remember that the devil has no authority over the children of God except what we let him have. Fear is one of the spirits he has working for him, but God has not given us a spirit of fear but of power, love, and a sound mind, as it says in 2 Timothy 1:7.

Fear is not a feeling or an emotion. It is a spiritual force, and although it can and does affect your emotions, it can be in operation even when you do not feel it. Never go by how you feel or by circumstances. Go by what God's word says. If we let the spirit of fear into our lives, it paralyzes us and prevents God from blessing us as he would like. But if you stay with God and stay on the word, you will stop the fear. Whenever fear takes over our lives, that is when faith ends. But you can overcome the spirit of fear in your life. If you meditate on the word of God, you can get rid of fear. You cannot immerse yourself in the word and be in fear at the same time. That is why it is so important to read God's word daily and to live it. We must fight the good fight of faith if we are to live the abundant life Jesus talked about. Fear is a spirit believers cannot tolerate in their lives. Before we were born again, we lived in Satan's kingdom, which was based on fear, but when we were born again, God delivered us out of the kingdom of Satan and into the kingdom of his dear son (Colossians 1:12-13). There is no fear in God's kingdom. In order to receive the blessings God has for us, we must get fear out of our lives, because if we do not, that fear will push the faith right out of our hearts. The way to get rid of fear in our lives is to saturate ourselves with the word of God and receive the mind of Christ. Then faith will come live in our hearts, and fear will be flushed out. When you spend time meditating on the word, you will begin to change your thinking and will think the way God thinks. That spirit of fear will have to go, and in its place you will have power, love, and a sound mind (2 Timothy 1:7).

Matthew 11:12 says, "And from the days of John the Baptist until now the kingdom of heaven suffers violence, and the violent take it by force." God has promised many blessing to his people, and we are entitled to them all, but just because God has promised them to us does not mean that we will possess them; it is up to us whether we will receive what God has promised us. Matthew 11:12 says the violent take it by force, and the devil has fooled many of God's people. He brings problems into their lives, and they say, "If God loved me, he would not have let this happen," but that is not a correct statement. You will have problems. Jesus said in John 15:19, "If you were of the world, the world would love its own. Yet because you are not of the world, but I chose you out of the world, therefore the world hates you." So we are going to have problems. The devil is not going to roll over and play dead while you take hold of the blessings in your life that God says belong to you if you are a born-again believer, and that is one of the reasons you do not see the power of God at work in most believers' lives. The devil knows that all he has to do is cause some problems in your life, and most people stop dead in their tracks and concentrate on the problems that the devil has brought to them. You notice I said "brought to them," because that is exactly the way it is: the devil brings problems into our lives, and instead of looking to God, we concentrate on what we are going through and play right into the devil's hands. But Jesus said in Matthew 6:25, "Therefore I say to you, do not worry about your life, what you will eat or what you will drink; nor about your body, what you will put on. Is not life more than food and the body more than clothing?" And then, in verse 33, he said, "but seek first the kingdom of God and His righteousness, and all things shall be added to you." God knows that we must eat, drink, and so on, but the key to these scriptures is found in verse 33. If we seek the kingdom

21

of God's righteousness, all these things we be added to us. People too often seek the gifts rather than the creator who gives us the gifts. God admonishes us in Luke 11:13, "If you then, being evil, know how to give good gifts to your children, how much more will your heavenly Father give the Holy Spirit to those who ask Him!" Think about what is more important to have—things, such as cars, houses, clothes and so on, or the Holy Spirit, God's power and authority in our lives. I do not know about you, but give me God's power, his authority his wisdom to help me live my life in this crazy, mixed-up world. God's power and wisdom are the most important things. There is a biblical example of this principle in the Old Testament concerning Solomon. Solomon was a young king in Israel, and he did not know how to be king so he prayed. And this is what he prayed in 1 Kings 3:8-9: "And your servant is in the midst of your people whom you have chosen, a great people, too numerous to be numbered or counted. Therefore give to your servant an understanding heart to judge your people, that I may discern between good and evil. For who is able to judge this great people of yours?" And in verses 10-14 it says,

> The speech pleased the Lord, that Solomon had asked this thing. Then God said to him: "Because you have asked this thing, and have not asked long life for yourself, nor have asked riches for yourself, nor have you asked the life of your enemies, but have asked for yourself understanding to discern justice, behold, I have done according to your words; see, I have given you a wise and understanding heart, so that there has not been anyone like you before you, nor shall any like you arise after you. And I have also given you what you have not asked: both riches and honor, so that there shall not be anyone like you among the kings all your days. So if you walk in my ways, to keep my statutes and my commandments, as your father David walked, then I will lengthen your days."

So Solomon did what the scripture says in Matthew 6:33—he sought the kingdom, God's wisdom and righteousness and all the other things, and material stuff was added to him as well. So we would do well to do the same. Nothing is more important than having a personal relationship with almighty God, because when we have a relationship with God, everything else in life is added to us. The devil tries hard to keep us looking at circumstances so that we don't focus our eyes on God, because he knows that God is the answer for anything that we might encounter in this life. Psalm 121:1-2 says, "I will lift up my eyes to the hills—From whence comes my help? My help comes from the Lord, who made heaven and earth." These scriptures tell us where our help comes from. The devil works overtime to get us focusing on what is going on in our lives. We need to make time to focus on God. Notice I said that we need to make time to focus on God. Do you remember the parable about the sower in Mark 4:3-9?

> "Listen! Behold, a sower went out to sow. And it happened, as he sowed, that some seed fell by the wayside; and the birds of the air came and devoured it. Some fell on stony ground, where it did not have much earth; and immediately it sprang up because it had no depth of earth. But when the sun was up it was scorched, and because it had no root it withered away. And some seed fell among thorns; and the thorns grew up and choked it, and it yielded no crop. But other seed fell on good ground and yielded a crop that sprang up, increased and produced: some thirtyfold, some sixty, and some a hundred. And he [Jesus] said to them, 'He who has ears to hear, let him hear!'

When Jesus was alone with his disciples, they asked him what the parable meant, and he explains in verse 14 of Mark 4,

> The sower sows the word. And these are the ones by the wayside where the word is sown. When they hear, Satan comes immediately and takes away the word that was sown in their hearts. These likewise are the ones sown on stony ground who, when they hear the word, immediately receive it with gladness; and they have no root in themselves, and

23

so endure only for a time. Afterward, when tribulation or persecution arises for the word's sake, immediately they stumble. Now these are the ones sown among thorns; they are the ones who hear the word, and the cares of this world, the deceitfulness of riches, and the desires for other things entering in choke the word, and it becomes unfruitful. But these are the ones sown on good ground, those who hear word, accept it, and bear fruit: some thirtyfold, some sixty, and some a hundred.

I have decided that I am the one that is on good ground that hears the word and receives it and bears fruit. Saints, do not let the devil steal the word out of your heart. To understand the parable better, please read Luke's account in Luke 8:5; he gives more detail. The point I am trying to make here is that we need to get into the word and let it change us. Look at Romans 12:1-2. "I beseech you therefore, brethren, by the mercies of God, that you present your bodies a living sacrifice, holy, acceptable to God, which is your reasonable service. And do not be conformed to this world, but be transformed by the renewing of your mind, that you may prove what is that good and acceptable and perfect will of God." It is God's will for us to be transformed or changed by his word and have our minds renewed. The devil is defeated. He has no authority over the blood-bought child of God. When Jesus died on that cross, he said, "It is finished," and that is what he meant. The devil's days are finished in our lives. We only have to believe and receive what Jesus has already done for us. God wants us to prosper in every area of our lives—spiritually, financially, socially, and physically. Read Joshua 1:8. "This Book of the Law [in other words, the Bible] shall not depart from your mouth, but you shall meditate in it day and night, that you may observe to do according to all that is written in it. For then you will make your way prosperous, and then you will have good success." God is telling us to read his word day and night, to meditate on it so we can live a prosperous life. That is his will for us, but notice what the devil wants for us. John 10:10 says, "The thief does not come except to steal, and to kill, and to destroy." To put it bluntly, the devil wants us dead. That is why Jesus came and died that horrible death. He did it all for us so we could live the abundant life that he provided for us. Another thing the devil has on his side is our flesh, and all flesh wants to do what it wants. The bible says in 1 Peter 2:11-12, "Beloved, I beg you as sojourners and pilgrims, abstain from fleshly lusts which was against the soul, having your conduct honorable among the Gentiles, that when they speak against you as evildoers, they may, by your good works which they observe, glorify God in the day of visitation." So not only do you have to contend with the devil, who wants you dead, but also with your flesh, which wars against your soul. That is why we are so dependent on God. There is no way we can make it in this world without him. But cheer up—we do not have to live without him. In Hebrews 13:5 he says he will never leave us for forsake us. That is a promise from God that we can depend on (all his promises are yes and amen). I remember years ago I had an issue concerning pleasing God. I loved him so much, but I had the feeling that somehow I would displease him. Fear was trying to rear its evil head in my life, and God spoke to my heart the scripture in 2 Timothy 1:7: "For God has not given us a spirit of fear, but of power and of love and of a sound mind." Then he gave me another scripture, Galatians 5:16: "I say then: Walk in the Spirit, and you shall not fulfill the lust of the flesh." If we are practicing spiritual activities, such as reading God's word, attending church activities, praying, and so forth, we will not be doing things that are displeasing to God. If our minds are on spiritual things, we do not have to be concerned about worldly matters. One of my favorite scriptures in the Bible is Isaiah 26:3: "You will keep him in perfect peace, Whose mind is stayed on you, Because he trusts in you." I want to encourage you to be strong in the Lord, and to be what God has called you to be, and above all to know who you are up against. Ephesians 6:12-18 says,

> For we do not wrestle against flesh and blood, but against principalities, against powers, against the rulers of the darkness of this age, against spiritual hosts of wickedness in the heavenly places. Therefore take up the whole armor of God, that you may be able to withstand in the evil day, and having done all, to stand. Stand therefore, having girded

your waist with truth, having put on the breastplate of righteousness, and having shod your feet with the preparation of the gospel of peace; above all, taking the shield of faith with which you will be able to quench all the fiery darts of the wicked one. And take the helmet of salvation, and the sword of the Spirit, which is the word of God; praying always with all prayer and supplication in the Spirit, being watchful to this end with all perseverance and supplication for all the saints.

The Bible tells us we are up against the devil, and it shows us what we are to do. If we just stay in the spirit and do things the way God tells us to, we can overcome anything that the devil brings against us.

CHAPTER 4

BEWARE OF LETTING STRIFE INTO YOUR LIFE

Paul writes in 2 Timothy 2:23-26, "But avoid foolish and ignorant disputes, knowing that they generate strife. And a servant of the Lord must not quarrel but be gentle to all, able to teach, patient, in humility correcting those who are in opposition, if God perhaps will grant them repentance, so that they may know the truth, and that they may come to their senses and escape the snare of the devil, having been taken captive by him to do his will." Based on this scripture, generating strife is a serious sin. We play right into the devil's hands when we get into strife. It says in 1 Corinthians 3:3, "For ye are yet carnal: for whereas there is among you envying, and strife, and divisions, are ye not carnal, and walk as men?" Carnal Christians are miserable people; they are born again and know enough about God not to sin deliberately, but they are not committed enough to stay out of sin. Strife will inhibit your ability to digest the meat of the word, and without that meat, you will not be able to grow into the strong, victorious Christians you should be. If you fuss and bicker with others, your spiritual growth will be stunted. You will remain a baby Christian, and the devil will run all over you. But do not stay a baby Christian. Do what Ephesians 4:15 says, "But, speaking the truth in love, may grow up in all things into Him who is the head—Christ." So stay out of strife and in the word of God.

I looked up the word *strife* and it means "a fight, quarrel, or struggle." The devil would like nothing better than to see God's people fighting with one another, because he knows that will keep you away from the will of God for your life, and his job is to do just that. James 3:14-16 says, "But if ye have bitter envying and strife in your hearts, glory not, and lie not against the truth. This wisdom descendeth not from above, but is earthly, sensual, devilish. For where envying and strife is, there is confusion and every evil work." The devil cannot stop the blessings of God from coming into your life, but he can delay them, and one way he does that is by getting us to fight with one another. This displeases God and gives the devil a foothold in our lives. So if you want the blessings of God to flow in your life, you must stay out of strife—it is a trick of the devil to stop the blessings of God from flowing in your life. Do not open the door to the devil in your life. Keep strife out of your life and enjoy the blessings God has provided for you and your loved ones. Strife has many dangers, but one of the most serious consequences of walking in strife is that it will hinder your prayers by robbing you of one of the greatest promises ever given to us. In Matthew 18:19, Jesus says, "Again I say unto you, That if two of you shall agree on earth as touching any thing that they shall ask, it shall be done for them of my Father which is in heaven." The devil hates agreement between believers. Agreement opens the windows of heaven to us, and it closes the door on every destructive thing he can do. Consequently, the devil will continually try to disrupt that agreement by causing strife and division in the two places where believers come together in the most powerful way: the family and the church. Decide today to stay out of strife and to walk in love, and if you do, the devil will not be able to burden your walk with God. So grow up in Christ; do not stay a baby. Get out of strife and into the word of God, and soon you will be the overcomers the word says you are.

Proverbs 6:16-19 says, "These six things doth the Lord hate: yea, seven are an abomination unto him: A proud look, a lying tongue, and hands that shed innocent blood, a heart that deviseth wicked imaginations, feet that be swift in running to mischief, A false witness that speaketh lies, and he that soweth discord among brethren." God looks at strife as a grave sin, and he mentions strife along with murder and lying. It is just as bad. You must determine in your heart that from now on if you see your brother sin, you will believe God for him and pray for him instead of talking about your brother's faults to everyone. The devil will try to get you to judge your brother, but 1 Corinthians 4:5 says, "Therefore judge nothing before the time, until the Lord come, who both will bring to light the hidden things of darkness, and will make manifest the counsels of the hearts: and then shall every man have praise of God."

Walk in love and you will always live in victory (praise God). I know that is easier said than done, but when you are tempted to get into strife by judging a fellow believer, just remember Romans 14:4: "Who are you to judge another's servant? To his own master he stands or falls. Indeed, he will be made to stand, for God is able to make him stand." Participating in strife in the church is one of the most dangerous of sins. When you are tempted to gossip and stir up strife, do not do it. Treat strife as you would a poisonous snake, because in the eyes of God, that is just how it is. Stay away from it!

James 3:14-16 says, "But if ye have bitter envying and strife in your hearts, glory not, and lie not against the truth. This wisdom descendeth not from above, but is earthly, sensual, devilish. For where envying and strife is, there is confusion and every evil work." This scripture tells us that strife is from the devil. That is why he wants us to argue and fight with one another and get offended or be critical of our brothers and sisters. It helps the devil's plan. He does not have to work hard to get us into strife, so do not play into his hands. Do as Galatians 6:1-2 says: "Brethren, if a man is overtaken in any trespass, you who are spiritual restore such a one in a spirit of gentleness, considering yourself lest you also be tempted. Bear one another's burdens, and so fulfill the law of Christ." We are all human beings; sometimes we do things and do not realize it. So we must do as that scripture says and bear one another's burdens if we are to please Christ. Do not give way to the devil. God has many blessings for his children, but one sure way to stop the flow of blessings in our lives is by getting into strife, because if you do, then the devil has won mastery over your life. He does not want you to enjoy the blessings of God. Even though you have a right to those blessings, staying in strife will stop them from coming to you. The devil does not want you to be healed, happy, and prosperous, because if you are, others may notice and want the same quality of life that you have. In order to stop that from happening, the devil tries to steal those blessings from you. But since he has no authority over you any more, he has to trick you into opening the door of your life to him. He will try to get you into strife with someone, because he knows that displeases God, and he will do anything he can to prevent you from fulfilling the will of God for your life. So make it a point to keep strife out of your life, and when you do mess up—and you will—be determined to be quick to repent, or the devil will gain a foothold in your life. You have an enemy. John 10:10 says, "The thief does not come except to steal, and to kill, and to destroy. I have come that they may have life, and that they may have it more abundantly." Not only will strife stop the flow of God's blessings into your life, but it also will stop you from being a spiritual, victorious Christian. In 1 Corinthians 3:1-3, Paul writes, "And I, brethren, could not speak unto you as unto spiritual, but as unto carnal, even as unto babes in Christ. I have fed you with milk, and not with meat: for hitherto ye were not able to bear it, neither yet now are ye able. For ye are yet carnal: for whereas there is among you envying, and strife, and divisions, are ye not carnal, and walk as men?" Carnal Christians are not happy people. It is true that they are born again and know enough about God not to enjoy sin, but they are not committed enough to God to stay out of sin. Living in strife will keep you a baby Christian—that is, a carnal Christian. You will not be able to digest the meat of the word, and without the meat of the word, you cannot grow into a strong, victorious Christian. When you are in strife, arguing and fighting, your spiritual growth will be stunted. You will remain a baby Christian with no power, and the devil will run all over you. So stay out of strife, and grow into a strong

Christian, one that the devil cannot handle. If you walk in love, you will always live in victory! If you are in a church where you feel the pastor has done wrong and you feel you do not want to follow him, leave that church and go to one with a pastor you can trust and respect. But do it quietly. Do not sow discord before you go. Wherever you go, be sure to go in love and guard against having strife. If you do, you will keep your faith strong and your blessings out of the devil's hands. In 2 Corinthians 4:7, Paul writes, "For we walk by faith, not by sight." This is one of the devil's greatest weapons that he uses against the body of Christ, and it has been very successful for him. Many Christians are led by what they feel instead of what the word says about a matter. They say things like, "I don't feel like going to church tonight. I'm tired." They ignore the scripture that says not to forsake gathering together (Hebrews 10:24-25). They go by what they feel and then wonder why they are not being blessed like the Lord says they should be. There is too much pride in the body of Christ. The Bible says pride comes before the fall. Everyone wants to pretend that everything is just fine when their lives are turned upside-down, and that is what the devil wants them to do. He does not want us to get the help we need; he wants us to go it alone. That way he can beat our brains out. We cannot live this Christian life by ourselves. Proverbs 18:1 says, "A man who isolates himself seeks his own desire; He rages against all wise judgment." We need one another. That is the only way we are going to make it. When we mature in Christ to the point of not being led by our feelings but by what God's word says, we are then and only then on our way to where God wants us to go. Then God can use us in his kingdom. Too many Christians are carnal Christians, led by what they feel. But how many know that that is not at all pleasing to God? Romans 8:13-14 says, "For if you live according to the flesh you will die, but if by the Spirit you put to death the deeds of the body, you will live. For as many as are led by the Spirit of God, these are sons of God." According to these verses, to be fleshly or carnally minded means death to us, but if we live by the Spirit and put to death the deeds of the body, we will live. I do not know about you, but I want to live, so I am determined that I will not be a carnal Christian. Let's go back to the scripture that says those who are led by the spirit of God (not their feelings) are the sons of God. Did you know you can be born-again Christians and not be led by the spirit of God? Only these who are led by the spirit of God are sons. We have a choice. We can be carnal Christians and be led by our feelings, or we can be sons of God and be led by the spirit of God.

CHAPTER 5

PROTECT THE ANOINTING

"The Spirit of the Lord God is upon me, because the Lord has anointed me to preach good tidings to the poor; he has sent me to heal the brokenhearted, to proclaim liberty to the captives, and the opening of the prison to those who are bound; to proclaim the acceptable year of the Lord, and the day of vengeance of our God; to comfort all who mourn." (Isaiah 61:1-2)

Jesus fulfilled this scripture, but did you know we are anointed just like Jesus if we are born again? This scripture also includes you and me. We are Jesus's feet and hands on this earth. He came and died and made a way for us to be reconciled back to God. Jesus is no longer here in the body, but he lives in every born-again believer's heart. The anointed one, Jesus, lives in us, so we must protect the anointing in us.

In Ephesians 4:1-3, Paul writes, "I, therefore, the prisoner of the Lord, beseech you to walk worthy of the calling with which you were called, with all lowliness and gentleness, with longsuffering, bearing with one another in love, endeavoring to keep the unity of the Spirit in the bond of peace." We are called to keep ourselves in a place where we can be anointed with the Holy Ghost and power so we can go everywhere healing all who are oppressed by the devil. It's the enormity that keeps us healed and prosperous and free of the devil's yoke. I refuse to do anything to stop the Spirit from working in my life. Philippians 4:13 says, "I can do all things through Christ which strengthen me." Paul was talking about the anointing. The anointing will empower you to prosper in spirit, soul, and body and in every area in your life.

The word *anoint* means "to pour on, smear all over, or rub into." When Jesus said the Lord had anointed him to preach good tidings to the poor, he was actually saying that he had come with the burden-removing, yoke-destroying power of the almighty God all over him to deliver people. So whatever bondage the devil is trying to hold you in, whether it be depressing poverty, sickness, fear, or whatever, you can be set free. The anointing destroys the yoke. The anointing is available to deliver you from every stronghold of the devil.

In John 14:12, Jesus says, "Most assuredly, I say to you, he who believes in me, the works that I do he will do also; and greater works than these he will do, because I go to my father" If you have made Jesus the lord of your life, the anointing is right there inside you.

Ever since the Fall, the devil has been using people as pack mules. He has clamped his yoke around their necks and burdened them down with fear, sickness, poverty, and anything else he can think of. To the natural eyes, it looks as though there will never be a way out. But thank God for Jesus! John 10:10 says that the devil comes to kill, steal, and destroy, but Jesus came to give us life and that more abundantly.

Jesus paid a great price for us, and he did not pay the price for our sins just so we could sail to heaven in the sweet by and by. He did it so you could be cleaned and be the temple of the Holy Spirit, who is the anointing. Jesus suffered, died, and rose again so that he could give birth to a new race of reborn men and women who would be equipped with his anointing. Jesus laid down his life so that he could raise up a race of believers who would walk on the earth doing not only the same works that he did but even greater works. Take hold of the anointing by expecting good things to happen in your life. Lay hold of the hope that is set before you in the promise of God. If God says you can be healed, expect your healing (1 Peter 2:24). If God says you can be prosperous, expect to prosper (3 John 1:3). Whatever God promises you in his word, believe it and stand on that word. Think about God's promises and meditate on them. Let them build an image inside you until you can see yourself healed, prosperous, or whatever you are believing God for, and if you will do that, I can tell you from experience that you will get bigger on the inside than you are on the outside. Your faith will be strong, and the devil himself will not be able to beat it out of you.

The anointing is very important in a born-again life, because without it we are just as weak as the unbelievers. Mark 6:5-6 says, "He could do no mighty work there, except that he laid hands on a few sick people and healed them, and He marveled because of their unbelief." Unbelief will stop the anointing from working in a person's life. Jesus could no miraculous works in his hometown because of unbelief. Faith is our anointing connection. When that connection is broken, there is nothing working to remove burdens and destroy yokes, which is what the anointing does.

Did you know that your love walk plays a big part in whether the anointing is working in your life? in other words, if you are not walking in love with people, the anointing is not being manifested in your life. So when the devil tries to get you to gossip or be in strife and hold unforgiveness against someone, do not fall for it. He is only trying to steal the anointing from your life. He knows that it is the anointing in a person's life that destroys bondage and yokes. The Bible says in Ephesians 6:10 that we are wrestling but not against flesh and blood. The devil tries to make you think you have a problem with people, but it is the devil you are up against.

In Matthew 5:44-45, Jesus says, "But I say to you, love your enemies, bless those who curse you, do good to those who hate you, and pray for those who spitefully use you and persecute you, that you may be sons of your Father in heaven; for he makes his sun rise on the evil and on the good, and sends rain on the just and on the unjust. For if you love those who love you, what reward have you? Do not even the tax collectors do the same?" It is very easy to love people who love you, but it gets a little difficult when you try to love people who do not love you. Maybe they gossip about you and cause strife. What do you do? The bible says to do good to those who hate you and pray for those who spitefully use and persecute you, that you may be sons of your Father in heaven. He makes his sun rise on the evil and on the good, so nobody is any better than anyone else. The only difference is that some know the will of God and do it, and others do not. Ephesians 2:1-2 says, "And you He made alive, who were dead in trespasses and sins, in which you once walked according to the course of this world, according to the prince of the power of the air, the spirit who now works in the sons of disobedience." We can see that before we were born again, we walked according to the course of this world. Sadly, some of us still do, but we do not have to. Jesus died on a cruel cross for the sins of mankind, but keep in mind that Jesus did not die just so we could go to heaven when we die; he died so we do not have to live depressed, joyless lives. He died so we could walk in divine health and have peace and prosperity and love for all mankind, just to name a few. So protect the anointing in your life, and remember that it is the anointing that destroys yokes and bondage in people's lives, and that is what God has called us to do. The more we study the word of God and build our faith in the anointing, the more manifestations we will see in our lives. I would like to tell you of an experience I had that shows just how important it is to protect the anointing in your life. There was a person who was upset with me for whatever reason, but I refused to let the devil disturb my peace, and I was not about to let him steal my anointing, because if I had let that happen I would not be able to help that person. So I just kept praying for her, speaking the word over this person's life, and asking God to help this person see how the devil was deceiving her. And after a few months of praying like that, I began to see changes in the person's life. The point I am trying to make here is that if you let the devil get you out of love and steal your peace, the anointing cannot work in your life. And remember, it is the anointing that destroys yokes. So fight for the anointing that is within you. Storm the gates of hell. They will not prevail against you.

We must protect the anointing at all cost, because without it there is nothing we can do. The devil know that; that is why he works so hard to try to stop the anointing from working in our lives. People must be delivered and set free, and only the yoke-destroying anointing of God will do that.

It says in 1 Peter 2:9, "But you are a chosen generation, a royal priesthood, a holy nation, His own special people, that you may proclaim the praises of Him who called you out of darkness into His marvelous light." The anointing is increasing in born-again believers throughout the world. They are flowing in the anointing and ministering to others, and signs and wonders are following. But even though we are seeing wonderful miracles, there are still a lot of religious people who say that things are not anointed. They say that Jesus was the only one truly anointed, but that is not true. It was never the Father's intention to anoint only Jesus with his power and leave it at that. One person could not get the work done, so God sent Jesus to the cross to die for mankind and then raised him from the dead. He wanted to open the way for us to become born again and to become a whole race of anointed men and women so that the world could be saved, delivered, and set free from the devil's bondage. That has been God's plan from the beginning. Through Jesus, the anointed one, he raised up a whole nation of kings and priests and called them his church. The verse in 1 Peter calls us a chosen generation, a royal priesthood. We are to be living proof that Jesus is alive and anointed with yoke-destroying power, because his anointing is on us. In the name of Jesus, we lay hands on the sick and they recover, we cast out devils, we speak the word of God in faith and set the captives free. We are not unworthy sinners as some religions teach. The Bible says we are joint heirs with Christ, sons of the most-high God.

CHAPTER 6

THE ANGELS ARE HERE TO SERVE YOU

Psalm 34:19 says, "Many are the afflictions of the righteous: but the Lord delivereth him out of them all." It does not matter what the devil uses against you to try to hinder your walk with God. We have ministering angels to help us to win the fight of faith.

Whatever you are facing today, your angels are there to protect you, so speak words of faith and put your angels to work for you. The angels assigned to you are bound by your words. They have been charged to listen to God's word—that is, to words of faith. So open your mouth and put your angels to work for you. Hebrews 1:14: "Are they not all ministering spirits sent forth to minister for those who will inherit salvation?" According to this scripture, the angels are there to help us to inherit (or receive) salvation. So put your angels to work for you, but remember to speak only words of faith, words that you want to come to pass in your life. If you speak words of faith, they will bring them to pass, but if you speak negative words, they cannot help you. Your angels are waiting on your faith-filled words. Let's look at Daniel 10:12. "Then he said to me, 'Do not fear, Daniel, for from the first day that you set your heart to understand, and to humble yourself before your God, your words were heard; and I have come because of your words." What we speak is very important. You can bless yourself with your words or you can curse yourself. Your words control your destroy, so be careful what you say. The key to receiving the desires of your heart is to make the words of your mouth agree with what you want. If you have spoken words of doubt and fear, you can quickly amend them, render those words powerless to come to pass, negate them in the name of Jesus, and reinstate what you want to come to pass.

Your words either put the angels to work or force them to step back, bow their heads, and fold their hands. Your angels are waiting for you to give them words to bring to pass. They have been sent forth to minister for you. Turn the angels loose to work on your behalf by continually speaking what you want to come to pass in your life. Your words put into motion your circumstances, the affairs of your life, the condition of your body, your acceptance or rejection by other people. God's word is his will. If your words are not your will, you will be disappointed in life, because your words will come to pass. When you confess the word of God over a situation, you put your angels to work.

Hebrews 1:14 says, "Are they not all ministering spirits sent forth to minister for them who shall be heirs of salvation?" The angels of God have been sent to minister for the heirs. "Christ hath redeemed us from the curse of the law, being made a curse for us . . . that the blessing of Abraham might come on the Gentiles through Jesus Christ; that we might receive the promise of the spirit through faith . . . and if ye be Christ's, then are ye Abraham's seed, and heirs according to the promise" (Galatians 3:13-29). If you have made Jesus the Lord of your life, then you are the seed of Abraham and heir to the blessing. That means that everything God promised Abraham belongs to you. It has been passed down to you through Jesus. Abraham's blessing is your inheritance. You are an heir. It has been willed to you by the word of God. And you need to read the will (which is the word of God) to find out what is rightfully due to you as the heir of Abraham. So stop reading the Bible like it is a book of stories. Read it and believe it like you would a will that details your inheritance. Enjoy the riches that are yours by virtue of the new birth. Discover for yourself that you truly are an heir to the limitless resources of the family of God!

God said to Abraham in Genesis 12:2, "I will make you a great nation; I will bless you, and make your name great; and you shall be a blessing." The word *bless,* according to the dictionary, means "to cause to prosper, to make happy, to bestow favor upon, to make successful." It was actually the blessing of God that made Abraham rich. It caused him to prosper wherever he went. I am determined that since I am an heir of Abraham, those words are just as true for me as they were for him. God keeps his promises. Whatever you need today, his word has a promise to cover your need. Find it and put your name in it. Confess it by faith and receive your inheritance as a seed of Abraham. Genesis 41 tells us that Abraham's great-grandson Joseph started out as a slave in the ungodly nation of Egypt, but because he was the seed of Abraham, just like you are, he ended up saving that nation from being destroyed by famine. He became the most powerful man in the nation next to Pharaoh himself. The entire country was blessed because of Joseph and his covenant with God. We were created to live above the circumstances of this world, so find out what is in the will or covenant and let God bless you the way he has always wanted too.

Since we are talking about how the angels serve us, let's look at a good example in Daniel 10:12-13: "Then he said to me, 'Do not fear, Daniel, for from the first day that you set your heart to understand, and to humble yourself before your God, your words were heard; and I [that is, an angel] have come because of your words. But the prince of the kingdom of Persia [that is, the devil] withstood me twenty-one days; and behold, Michael, one of the chief princes, came to help me, for I had been left alone there with the kings of Persia." This is a great example for us. When we get to the place in God where we are one with him, he hears us the first day, and the answer is on the way. I like that, but always keep in mind that the devil will always try to stop your blessings from God. But this is where we come in; we must have faith in what God has said and not let doubt, fear, or unbelief get in the way. We must speak what God says. God says his word will not return void; it will accomplish what he has said. Isaiah 55:9-11 says,

For as the heavens are higher than the earth, so are my ways higher than your ways, and my thoughts than your thoughts. For as the rain comes down, and the snow from heaven, and do not return there, but water the earth, and make it bring forth and bud, that it may give seed to the sower and bread to the eater, so shall my word be that goes forth from my mouth; it shall not return to me void, but it shall accomplish what I please, and it shall prosper in the thing for which I sent it.

So if God says something, it will come to pass just as he said. The problem with us it that we put limits on things, and if they have not manifested when we think they should, we start thinking that God did not hear us. But on the contrary, delay does not mean denial. Did you know that sometimes God also allows things to happen to us? But God's grace is sufficient for whatever we go through. In my own personal life, when I have prayed about a matter and it has not come to pass as quickly as I anticipated, it has only made my faith stronger and drawn me closer to God. It just made me pray and praise that much more. I like to give God praise before the manifestation, because I know it is just a matter of time before what I am believing for comes to pass. When you get to the place in God where you believe his word no matter how long it takes or what circumstances try to stop your blessings from coming to pass, then and only then are you in the place where God desires you to be. And that is where God can really do something in your life and in the lives of your loved ones. Keep in mind that it is not about us but about all those people out there who need God in their lives. Delay does not mean denial, because sometimes God may have to do a work in us before he can answer our prayers. So just be patient, and what you are believing God for will come to pass in due season.

CHAPTER 7

IF GOD BE FOR YOU, WHO CAN BE AGAINST YOU?

2 Chronicles 16:9 says, "For the eyes of the Lord run to and fro throughout the whole earth, to shew himself strong in the behalf of them whose heart is perfect toward him." The Father is looking for people to show himself strong in their lives. He wants to bless you. If you read the Bible, you will see that ever since the world began, God has been looking for people who have faith and obedience who will allow him to bless them right here on the earth. He wants to demonstrate his power in their lives, so be obedient to God and let him demonstrate his power and faithfulness on your behalf and bless you the way he wants to. If you want to see how blessed God wants us to be, just look at the Garden of Eden. That was God's perfect will for man. Genesis 2:8-9 says, "The Lord God planted a garden eastward in Eden, and there he put the man whom he had formed. And out of the ground the Lord God made every tree grow that is pleasant to the sight and good for food. The tree of life was also in the midst of the garden, and the tree of the knowledge of good and evil." So you see, God wanted us to live a good life. All man had to do was obey the word of God. God has not

changed his mind about wanting to bless his people, but we must obey his word in order to benefit from all the things God has prepared for us. Do not listen to the devil like Adam and Eve and lose out on God's blessings for you. When the devil comes into your personal garden, tell him to get out. Even though God wants good for you, the devil does not want you to get what God has for you. So you have to fight to get what belongs to you, but it is not a physical fight; it is a spiritual fight. Ephesians 6:10-13 says, "Finally, my brethren, be strong in the Lord and in the power of His might. Put on the whole armor of God, that you may be able to stand against the wiles of the devil. For we do not wrestle against flesh and blood, but against principalities, against powers, against the rulers of the darkness of this age, against spiritual hosts of wickedness in the heavenly places. Therefore take up the whole armor of God, that you may be able to withstand in the evil day, and having done all, to stand." We are an army, and we are in a war, but it is not against flesh and blood. The devil would love for you to believe that you are up against people, because if you do, you will not put up a fight against him; you will be too busy trying to fight against people instead of doing what God commands you to do. Let's look at Matthew 5:44. "But I say to you, love your enemies, bless those who curse you, do good to those who hate you, and pray for those who spitefully use you and persecute you, that you may be sons of your Father in heaven; for He makes His sun rise on the evil and on the good, and sends rain on the just and on the unjust." God loves us all; the only difference is that some of us take advantage of that privilege and others do not. But it is God's will for all of us to be blessed and prosper. Isaiah 1:19 says, "If you are willing and obedient, you shall let the good of the land." We must be determined to get what God has for us. When Jesus died for us, it was not only for our salvation. I looked up the word *salvation*, and it means "spiritual rescue from sin and death; redemption." Jesus has redeemed us not only from sin but also from sickness, poverty, and a host of other things. Sickness and poverty are under the curse. As born-again children of God, we are no longer under the curse. Galatians 3:13 says, "Christ has redeemed us from the curse of the law, having become a curse for us (for it is written, 'Cursed is everyone who hangs on a tree')." Because of what Jesus did, we no longer are under the curse. Jesus became that curse in our place, so I refuse to live under the curse of sin, sickness, poverty, and the like.

I am determined to have all that Jesus died for me to have. Galatians 3:29 says if you are Christ's, then you are Abraham's seed and heirs according to the promises. As born-again believers, you and I are God's people just as the Israelites were. Since we are Christ, then, we are Abraham's seed and heirs according to the promise. We should expect God to anoint the works of our hands. We can expect him to bless us and give us the power to get wealth. Deuteronomy 8:18 says, "And you shall remember the Lord your God, for it is he who gives you the power to get wealth, that he may establish his covenant which he swore to your Fathers, as it is this day." So it is God's will to prosper his people. It is part of the benefit package of Christ's death on our behalf. It says in 3 John 2 "Beloved, I wish above all things that thou mayest prosper and be in health, ever as thy soul prospereth." It is important to grasp what the apostle John was saying here. Notice that he did not just say, "I want you to prosper." He said, "I want you to prosper as your soul prospers." He tied financial prosperity to the prosperity of the mind, will, and emotions. God's plan is for us to grow financially as we grow spiritually. He knows it is dangerous to put great wealth into the hands of someone who is immature and does not know how to handle the money. If you go back to Deuteronomy 8:18, the last part of the verse says he gives us wealth to establish his covenant on the earth. The preaching of the good news is the most important thing we have to do. We must get souls saved, but God also knows we need money to do that, so we prosper financially as our souls prosper spiritually. You can see that in the lives of people who have acquired financial riches through this world's system but are not rich toward God. In most cases, such riches just help people to die younger and in more misery than if they had been poor. We can see from that phenomenon that God wants us to increase financially at the same pace we increase spiritually. He wants us to outgrow our fleshly foolishness so our prosperity will bring us blessing and not harm. Jeremiah 29:11 says, "For I know the thoughts that I think toward you, says the Lord, thoughts of peace and not of evil, to give you a future and a hope." Never try to build a house without first laying the foundation. I do not care how eager you are to get it finished, how excited you are about filling it with furniture and decorating it all just right; take time to put down a solid foundation first. If you do not, that house will be so unstable it will soon come tumbling down. The same is true of a relationship with God. We first must get to know God and build a relationship with him. Then all the promises he died for us to have will be ours. Matthew 6:33 says to seek the kingdom first and his righteousness, and all these things shall be added to us. Keep in mind that the foundation of prosperity is a continual lifestyle built on the word of God. It is doing whatever God tells us to do, thinking whatever he tells us to think, and saying whatever he tells us to say. Godly prosperity is the result of putting God's word first in your life both by hearing it and by doing it, so start building now!

God wants the best for us. That is why God sent Jesus to die for us—to ensure that we would have a wonderful life. In John 10:10, Jesus says, "The thief does not come except to steal, and to kill, and to destroy. I have come that they may have life, and that they may have it more abundantly." It is God's will that we live a good life, but the enemy of our souls, the devil, wants us to live a defeated life. But know that "greater is he that is in you than he that is in the world." When sickness and pain comes against your body, do not just accept that. Let the devil know that Jesus took your sickness and pain and that by the stripes of Jesus you are healed. Some Christians think that if we say that by the stripes of Jesus we are healed and yet there continues to be bodily pain, we are living in denial. But just the opposite is true! We are not denying that the pain is there; we are just denying the right of that pain to stay in our bodies. Those who have been born again are now Christians in Christ, and we have rights and privileges. The bible talks about that in Deuteronomy 28. There it tells us that if we are obedient to God's word, we will be blessed; but if we are disobedient, we will be cursed. Sickness and disease are under the curse, and Jesus died on the cross and became a curse for us. Galatians 3:13 says, "Christ has redeemed us from the curse of the law, having become a curse for us (for it is written, 'Cursed is everyone who hangs on a tree')." Jesus hung on the tree and took our sickness and disease, and we do not have to take it anymore. We have authority over sickness and disease in Jesus's name, and we must say so. If we do not, the devil will run all over us and keep us sick, worried, and living a defeated life in spite of our rights as Christians. If you never exercise your rights as a child of God, you will live a defeated life while you are here on this earth. What a shame, when Jesus came and died so you could have a good life. This is the reason God wanted me to write this book—so his children would know who they are in Christ. In Jesus's name, we have a great deal of authority, and when we realize that, the devil's days will be over in our lives.

The devil wants you to continue being ignorant of him, but 1 Peter 5:8 says "Be sober, vigilant; because your adversary the devil walks about like a roaring lion, seeking whom he may devour." Well, I am whom he wants to devour. I know my rights in Christ. I am blood-bought. Jesus died for me. He took my sickness and disease, and by his stripes I am healed. If the devil can keep you ignorant of those facts, then he has you right where he wants you. But I refuse to let Jesus's death on my behalf be in vain. I will have everything that Jesus died for me to have. Abundant life belongs to me, and I receive it now in Jesus's name.

God never meant for his people to live in lack and want. That is why God made a covenant with Abraham. God said that in Abraham, all the nations would be blessed (Genesis 2:3). As God's people, we need to know what the covenant says. A covenant is between two people. One has to do his part, and the other one has to do his part. God's part in the covenant is to prosper us in spirit, soul, and body as well as financially; but our part is not to seek after prosperity but to seek first his kingdom, his way of doing and being right. Matthew 6:33 says Abraham's blessing is your inheritance, and it has been willed to you by the word of God, so read the will, which is the word of God, and find out what rightfully belongs to you. Hosea 4:6 says God's people are destroyed for a lack of knowledge. You have heard it said that what you do not know will not hurt you, but I say that what you do not know can kill you. That is why there is so much struggling in the body of Christ: people just do not know their covenant rights. For example, Galatians 3:13 says we have been redeemed from the curse. Lack and poverty are under the curse, and we have been redeemed from that, so why are so many Christians still living in lack and poverty? It is because there is no revelation knowledge of what the covenant is and what it can do in our lives. Here's an example from my own life. I was going through a lot of stuff, but I had the wrong mind-set. (You know that the devil tries to keep you with the wrong mind-set.) I was going through stuff, and I kept saying, "This is making me stronger in the Lord," and one day I got a revelation about my situation. At the time I did not have a job, and then one day it hit my spirit: What are you thinking? You are a covenant child with rights and privileges.

Then I saw the situation differently. I started talking to my situation, and I have not stopped yet. I also let the devil know that I have a covenant with God, not him, and that I was supposed to have a job. I am supposed to have money to pay my bills and support the preaching work; that is my destiny. And when I started thinking things like that, things started to change. I got a job, and things are getting better every day. But nothing happened until my thinking changed. God has so much in store for his people, but we have to get our minds renewed. How we see ourselves is what determines what we will have in life. If you see yourself living in lack, sickness, and depression, that is how it is going to be for you. But if you see yourself as God sees you, as the righteousness of God and more than a conqueror in Christ Jesus, your life will change. Agree with who God says you are, and you will never be the same. I am a living testimony to that. Did you know that it is not God's will for you, his children, to struggle and barely make ends meet? John 10:10 says, "The thief does not come except to steal, and to kill, and to destroy. I have come that they may have life, and that they may have it more abundantly." That is the reason Jesus came and died—so that we could live an abundant life now while we are here on the earth, not when we go to heaven. We need the abundant life here on the earth, not in heaven. When I say the struggle is over for the body of Christ, everyone is not going to receive that, but everyone can. Those who have had all that they are going to take from the devil will come to this revelation: the struggle is over. The devil is defeated, and it is time that we not only say that but also put that devil under our feet where he belongs. The abundant life that Jesus died for us to have is available for us right now, but it is up to us whether we will receive it or not.

The problem in the body of Christ is that we do not know the authority we have in Jesus. In Luke 10:13, when Jesus sent the seventy disciples out, he said, "Behold, I give you the authority to trample on serpents and scorpions, and over all the power of the devil, and nothing shall by any means hurt you." When the body of Christ receives the revelation that we are victorious in Christ Jesus and that the devil is a defeated foe, only then will we put him in his place (which is under our feet) and take back everything he has stolen from us—our joy, our peace, our finances, and so forth. Then his days of dominating us will be over. Jesus came and died so we could have the abundant life. My heart goes out to people who live their lives in fear and depression without any joy and peace at all. and they don't have to live that way any longer because Jesus made a way for us when he died on the cross.

Another blessing that most members of the body of Christ are not experiencing in their lives is rest. Hebrews 4:1, 8-10 says, "Therefore since a promise remains of entering His rest, let us fear lest any of you seem to have come short of it . . . For if Joshua had given them rest, then He would not afterward have spoken of another day. There remains therefore a rest for the people of God. For he who has entered His rest has himself also ceased from his works as God did from His." The last statement in this verse is powerful. It says that if we have entered God's rest, then we cease from our works. Why are we constantly trying to do something for God when all God wants us to do is rest in him and put our whole trust in him to take care of us? Did you know that is part of the promise from God—that we enter into his rest? When we do, we have ceased from our own works, which include doubt and unbelief and fear, to name a few. When the body of Christ really understands who they are in Christ and how powerful we are in Jesus's name, our days of struggle will be truly over. Then and only then will we put the devil under our feet where he belongs. Only then can we live the abundant life that Jesus wants us to live. This is not about us. There is a world out there where people are dying and going to Hell because God's people have not taken their place in God and positioned themselves to take back everything the devil has stolen from us—our marriages, our children, our peace, our joy, and our finances. I do not know about you, but I have had enough, and I am not going to take any more. In Jesus's name, I am taking it all back, because Jesus said I could. That is why he came.

CHAPTER 8

ENTER GOD'S REST

Hebrews 4:9-11: "There remains therefore a rest for the people of God. For he who has entered his rest than himself also ceased from his works as God did from his . . . Let us therefore be diligent to enter that rest, lest anyone fall according to the same example of disobedience."

Once you enter into the rest of God, the scripture says you cease from your works. I looked up the word *cease*, and it means "to end or to stop." When you enter into God's rest, it is the most amazing experience of your life. As long as we are here on this earth, we are going to have problems; the devil will see to that. But when you learn to rest in God and cast your cares on him, you are in the kingdom. Remember when they arrested Jesus and took him before Pontius Pilate and Pilate told Jesus be had the power to release him or crucify him, Jesus told Pilate, "You would have no power over me at all if it had not been given from above." Jesus never got bent out of shape. Jesus knew what he had come to this earth to do, and he also knew his kingdom was not of this world. Once we learn that, we will just rest in the Lord, and the devil's days will be over in our lives,

In 1 Corinthians 10:13, Paul writes, "There hath no temptation taken you but such as is common to man: but God is faithful, who will not suffer you to be tempted above that ye are able; but will with the temptation also make a way to escape, that ye may be able to bear it." Tradition reads this verse as saying God will let you suffer individually in each trial to your boiling point, and when he is sure that you can take no more, he will provide an answer that you can tolerate. I used to believe that. In John 4:32, Jesus said, "You will know the truth, and the truth will set you free." Thank God.

The devil is bound by the laws of God. He can bring no trial to you that you cannot overcome with God's word. When it says God will not allow the devil to go beyond the limit he has in the earth to try your faith (God will try our faith), but if we will just rest in him, there is nothing the devil can do to us. At the end of that passage, it says God will make a way "that ye may be able to bear it"—in other words, God will enable you to endure the devil's pressure to yield to circumstances without surrendering to that pressure. When the devil tempts you to back off from God's word, he is trying your faith. We have the opportunity to prove that we believe God's word is true. James 1:2-4 says, "My brethren, count it all joy when you fall into various trials, knowing that the testing of your faith produces patience. But let patience have its perfect work, that you may be perfect and complete, lacking nothing." My favorite verse in God's word is Isaiah 26:3: "You will keep him in perfect peace, whose mind is stayed on you, because he trusts in you." When our minds are stayed on God, it is hard for the devil to get into our lives. In my personal life, I do just that; no matter what I am doing, I keep my mind on God. That makes it hard for the devil to get into your life. We all have cares in this life, but we must do what 1 Peter 5:6-7 says: "Therefore humble yourselves under the mighty hand of God, that he may exalt you in due time, casting all your care upon Him, for He cares for you."

God wants us all to come to the place where we rest in him. Everyone will not get there, but everyone can. Hebrews 3:12-19 says,

> Beware, brethren, lest there be in any of you an evil heart
> of unbelief in departing from the living God; but exhort
> one another daily, while it is called 'Today,' lest any of you

be hardened through the deceitfulness of sin. For we have become partakers of Christ if we hold the beginning of our confidence steadfast to the end, while it is said: 'Today, if you will hear His voice, do not harden your hearts as in the rebellion.' For who, having heard, rebelled? Indeed, was it not all who came out of Egypt, led by Moses? Now with whom was He angry forty years? Was it not with those who sinned, whose corpses fell in the wilderness? And to whom did He swear that they would not enter His rest, but to those who did not obey? So we see that they could not enter in because of unbelief.

When you get to the place where you are resting in God (and remember that we are commanded to enter the rest of God), it is a wonderful place to be when you have every confidence in your God and you know that you know that you know that God loves you. There is not a better feeling in the world.

I want to share my personal testimony, which shows how cunning the devil is and how he will try his hardest to get you to stop resting in God. I was going along fine just resting and trusting God when something happened in my life that made me wonder where God was, and I even became frustrated with God. (The enemy loves that.) When someone is being used by God, that person makes a big dent in the kingdom of darkness, the devil tries very hard to make that person stop trusting God. Actually, he is trying to steal that person's anointing. Remember that the anointing is what destroys yokes and bondage in a person's life. For a few weeks, I stopped reading the word and going to church as I used too. I was playing right into the devil's hands. Then one morning I woke up (thank God for his mercy and grace), and I prayed to God and asked him to restore my love for reading the word and going to church, and he did. I also asked God to give me back my desire to help others get delivered and set free from bondage. That experience has helped me to be more aware of just how important it is not to become offended and to read and meditate on the word continually. When we are going through problems is when we need it the most. We have an enemy. The devil does not want you to trust and rest in God. Remember that according to John 10:10, the devil is the thief who "cometh but to steal, and to kill, and to destroy."

Hebrews 4:1-2 says, "Let us therefore fear, lest, a promise being left us of entering into his rest, any of you should seem to come short of it. For unto us was the gospel preached, as well as unto them: but the word preached did not profit them, not being mixed with faith in them that heard it." Verses 9-11 of the same chapter go on to say, "There remains therefore a rest for the people of God. For he who has entered His rest has himself also ceased from his works as God did from His. Let us therefore be diligent to enter that rest, lest anyone fall according to the same example of disobedience." Did you know that God's word commands us to enter into his rest and then stay there? Psalm 37:7 says, "Rest in the Lord, and wait patiently for him; Do not fret because of him who prospers in his way, because of the man who brings wicked schemes to pass." I looked up the word *rest* in *Webster's New World Dictionary*, and one definition was "absence of motion." I really like that definition, because a lot of God's people are always trying to do works to please him, when salvation is a gift from God. Another definition is "to cease from works." Let's go back to Hebrews 4:9-10. "There remains therefore a rest for the people of God. For he who has entered His rest has himself also ceased from his works as God did from His."

God's will is for all his children to enter into his rest. He wants us to trust him and rest from our own works. Let us believe what he says in his word concerning us and stand on that word until God brings it to pass in our lives, and when we come to that point in our lives, our days of struggling will be over, because we will have learned to rest in God and trust him to take care of us. And that is what he has always wanted us to do.

CHAPTER 9

$\sim$

BECOME A DOER OF THE WORD AND NOT A HEARER ONLY

What does it profit, my brethren, if someone says he has faith but does not have works? Can faith save him? If a brother or sister is naked and destitute of daily food, and one of you says to them, "Depart in peace, be warmed and filled," but you do not give them the things which are needed for the body, what does it profit? Thus also faith by itself, if it does not have works, is dead. But someone will say, "You have faith, and I have works." Show me your faith without your works, and I will show you my faith by my works. You believe that there is one God. You do well. Even the demons believe—and tremble! But do you want to know, O foolish man, that faith without works is dead? (James 2:14-20)

We can see from these scriptures that believing is not enough. The demons believe God—and tremble. It goes on to say that faith without works is dead. If we do not have faith, we cannot please God. Right along with our faith, we must have works. When you think of works, you think of doing something. Read Hebrews 4:1-2: "Let us therefore fear, lest, a promise being left us of entering into his rest, any of you should seem too come short of it. For unto us was the gospel preached as well as unto them." This passage is speaking of the Israelites, and it goes on to say, "But the word preached did not profit them, not being mixed with faith in them that heard it." And then, in verse 9, "There remaineth therefore a rest to the people of God. For he that entered into his rest, he also hath ceased from his own works, as God did from his. Let us labour therefore to enter into that rest, lest any fall after the same example of unbelief." The scripture shows us here that unbelief is a work. And that is why the Israelites did not enter into the promised land—because of unbelief. When Moses told the people that God had given them the land, he sent out twelve spies, but all of them except for Joshua and Caleb came back with a negative report. Ten of the spies were unbelievers. God said he had given them the land, but they did not believe him. We can have works of faith or works of unbelief.

We have another example of someone who displayed his works in James 2:21-25. "Was not Abraham our father justified by works, when he offered Isaac his son upon the altar? . . . Ye see then how that by works a man is justified, and not by faith only. Likewise also was not Rahab the harlot justified by works, when she had received the messengers, and had sent them out another way?" Abraham and Rahab not only had faith but also had works to go along with their faith. Abraham offered Isaac his son upon the altar, showing his faith in God. Similarly, Rahab received the spies who came to her, and she had faith—she believed that God would give them the land as he said. She protected them from the king, and the Bible says she sent them out another way. She had works to go along with her faith. That is the only way we can receive anything from God.

Jesus gives us another example of how important it is to be doer of the word. He talks about two men, one wise and one foolish. Here it is in Matthew 7:24-27:

> Therefore whoever hears these sayings of Mine, and does
> them, I will liken him to a wise man who built his house
> on the rock: and the rain descended, the floods came, and

the winds blew and beat on that house; and it did not fall, for it was founded on the rock. But everyone who hears these sayings of Mine, and does not do them, will be like a foolish man who built his house on the sand: and the rain descended, the floods came, and the winds blew and beat on that house; and it fell. And great was its fall."

These scriptures demonstrate that if we want to be wise (and we all do), we must not only hear the sayings of God but also do them. And if we do, then when the storms of life come against us, we will stand. In other words, we will not back off from God's word. It says that the wise man's house was built on a rock—that is, on Jesus Christ. But the foolish man hears the sayings of God but does not do them, and when problems come, he is not able to stand on the word. Just hearing God's word does not help you unless you also do what it says. We must not only be hearers of the word but doers as well.

Did you know you could deceive yourself just by going to church, listening to the word, and not doing anything about it? The devil does not mind if you go to church or even read the word. His problem comes when you start applying the word in your life. Look at James 1:22-25: "But be doers of the word, and not hearers only, deceiving yourselves. For if anyone is a hearer of the word and not a doer, he is like a man observing his natural face in a mirror; for he observes himself, goes away, and immediately forgets what kind of man he was. But he who looks into the perfect law of liberty and continues in it, and is not a forgetful hearer but a doer of the work, this one will be blessed in what he does." Like the houses of the wise man and the foolish man, the word can become one thing for one person and something entirely different for another. The reason for that is that God's word is alive. The word of God gives life to those who apply it in their lives. The bible likens the word to a lamp. The word of God has the supernatural life within it to fulfill all of the promises of God in our lives. When you hear the word and receive it in your heart, it springs up in different ways: salvation, healing, prosperity, joy, peace—whatever you need in your life. Whatever you need in your life, go to the word, find a promise to stand on (something God has promised you in his word), and begin planting that seed (or word) in your heart. Say the promise over and over as you let that word take root inside of you. Let the word become real to you and then watch it come to life.

Many Christians really do not understand how important works are in conjunction with their faith. Mark 11:2 says that "whosoever shall say unto this mountain, Be thou removed, and be thou cast into the sea; and shall not doubt in his heart, but shall believe that those things which he saith shall come to pass; he shall have whatsoever he saith." Remember what the Bible says about the heart in Jeremiah 17:9. It says the heart is deceitful; who can know it? Note that this verse says not only that you have to believe but that you have to say. You have to say what you want to come to pass. I hope you are beginning to see that just having faith in God's word is not enough.

It is true that we must have faith. Hebrews 11:16 says without faith, it is impossible to please God. But we have to go beyond just faith. Patience is also very important. Hebrews 10:36 says, "For ye have need of patience, that after ye have done the will of God ye might receive the promise." It is true that faith is important, but patience is just as important. When you exercise faith in something God has promised you, you also need to have patience until it is manifested in your life. John 10:10 says that Satan comes to kill, steal, and destroy, but Jesus comes so we can have life and that more abundantly. Jesus wants us to exercise faith in his word so we can have the abundant life he died for us to have. Satan, on the other hand, wants to steal our blessings, and so far he has been pretty successful. When we, the body of Christ, just come to church and hear God's word and do not apply it in our lives, it does not help anyone. But when we go a step further, we are like the wise man in Matthew 7:24 who built his house on a rock, which was Jesus, and the floods and winds came, but the house did not fall, for it was founded on a rock. God is very pleased with us when we not only hear his word but also act on it; it gives him pleasure.

Psalm 37:25 says God takes pleasure in the prosperity of his servants, so God wants us to prosper and enjoy to the full all that Jesus died for us to have. That verse makes it clear that God takes pleasure when his people prosper. But the only way we can prosper in the things of God is to hear and do what the word of God says. John 8:31-32 says,

"Then said Jesus to those Jews which believed on him, If ye continue in my word, then are ye my disciples indeed; and ye shall know the truth, and the truth shall make you free." The more we believe the word and apply it in our lives, the freer we are. To help you understand that better, let's look at 1 John 3:8. "He that committeth sin is of the devil; for the devil sinneth from the beginning. For this purpose the Son of God was manifested, that he might destroy the works of the devil." So another reason that Jesus came was so that he could destroy the works of the devil. Do you realize that if Jesus had not come and destroyed the works of the devil, we would still be serving the devil? I do not know about you, but that makes me happy (praise God). Because of what Jesus did, the devil has no more authority over us. He wants us to think he does, but he does not. He only deceives people. Remember that he comes to steal, kill, and destroy, but he cannot do that unless you let him.

Believers who hear the word and apply that word in their lives are tough for the devil to handle. He counts on us just being hearers of the word. But God told Joshua in Joshua 1:8 that if he meditated on the word day and night, he would make his way prosperous and he would have good success. The devil cannot stop the blessings of God from coming into your life, but he can delay them. One way he does that is by getting you to hear the word without applying it in your life. I do not know about you, but I am thankful that Jesus came and died for our sins so we could be reconciled back to the Father. When Adam gave in to sin, Satan became our father, but when Jesus came and died for us, all that changed. Every day I wake up and thank God for what Jesus did. I get happy just thinking about it. No longer is Satan our father, no longer does he lead us around like pack mules to do his bidding. The devil is under my feet, and that is where he will stay (praise God). Thank you, Jesus, for giving us victory over the devil. As soon as the saints realize who they are in Christ and understand the power and authority that Christ won and gave back to us, the devil's days will be numbered in our lives. And he knows it; he just hopes you never realize it, because he knows that then it will all be over for him. Romans 12:1-2 says, "I beseech you therefore, brethren, by the mercies of God, that ye present your bodies a living sacrifice, holy, acceptable unto God, which is your reasonable service. And be not conformed to this world: but be ye transformed by the renewing of your mind, that ye may prove what is that good, and acceptable, and perfect, will of God." With the mind-set that most people have, we will never be able to please God. But once we do what Paul is talking about and have our minds renewed that we may prove the good, and acceptable, and perfect will of God, once we renew our minds and think like God thinks, it is over for the devil. And he knows it. That is why he tries so hard to keep us out of the word of God—so we won't have our minds renewed. Christians who do not know what the word of God says about them are unable to live and enjoy all the privileges that Christ died for us to have. Their minds have not been renewed to walk in the Spirit; therefore they continue to walk after the dictates of their flesh, so whatever they feel like doing, they do. The mind that has not been renewed to the word of God does not even realize it has a choice except to receive whatever the devil is offering it. They do not even realize that they have an alternative. And it is really sad, because a believer has at his disposal all of the spiritual weapons in heaven's arsenal, but if his mind has never been renewed to the word of God, he does not even know that, much less how to use those weapons. He is at the devil's mercy, and the devil has no mercy. Hosea 4:6 talks about how God's people are destroyed for a lack of knowledge. You owe it to yourself, you owe it to God, to find out who you are in Christ and put the devil where he belongs, which is under your feet. That is why there are so many sick, broke, and depressed Christians: they do not know who they are in Christ and that they have to apply the word of God in their lives—not just hear what the word says, but do it. Joshua 1:8 says, "This book of the law shall not depart out of thy mouth; but thou shalt meditate therein day and night, that thou mayest observe to do according to all that is written therein: for then thou shalt make thy way prosperous, and then thou shalt have good success." Not only should we not let God's word depart from our mouths, we must also meditate or think deeply about the word and do all that is written therein so we can be prosperous, and then we will have good success. Just hearing the word does not bring success; it's meditating on and doing the word that does that. The word works, but we must work the word. The enemy knows what will happen if we meditate on the word day and night; that is why he tries so hard to get us involved in everything except reading and applying the word of God in our lives.

On a personal note, I am so happy in the Lord. I love to read God's word, and the more I do, the more I want to. When you get like that, you are tough for the devil to handle, but before I knew who I was in Christ, the devil had me in fear as he does a lot of Christians today, deceiving them and making them think he is all that when really he is only a defeated foe. Jesus came and stripped the devil of all the power and authority that Adam gave him. Hebrews 2:14-15 says, "Forasmuch then as the children are partakers of flesh and blood, he also himself likewise took part of the same; that through death he might destroy him that had the power of death, that is, the devil; And deliver them who through fear of death were all their lifetime subject to bondage." We are free, but a lot of us do not know that yet. John 8:31-32: "Then said Jesus to those Jews which believed on him, if ye continue in my word, then are ye my disciples indeed; and ye shall know the truth, and the truth shall make you free." I cannot express to you enough how important reading God's word is. The more you read, the more you learn, and the more you apply God's word in your lives, the freer you are in Christ. You will know the truth, and the truth will make you free. This book is about Christ's death not being in vain. He died so you could have life and that more abundantly. That is why he came. He does not want you to be sick, depressed, broke, and all those other things. Remember what Jesus says in John 10:10: "The thief cometh not, but for to steal, and to kill, and to destroy; I am come that they might have life, and that they might have it more abundantly." I am on a mission. I am on my way to heaven by the grace of God. I am going to take as many as I can with me.

John 3:16 says, "For God so loved the world, that he gave his only begotten Son, that whosoever believeth in him should not perish, but have everlasting life." Jesus's death on my behalf was not in vain. My prayer for you is that you get into God's word, meditate on it, and apply it in your lives. Put the devil where he belongs: under your feet. He has no authority over you but what you give him; he can do only what you let him do. The last verse I will use in this chapter is 1 Peter

5:7-10: "Casting all your care upon him; for he careth for you. Be sober, be vigilant; because your adversary the devil, as a roaring lion, walketh about, seeking whom he may devour: Whom resist steadfast in the faith, knowing that the same afflictions are accomplished in your brethren that are in the world. But the God of all grace, who hath called us unto his eternal glory by Christ Jesus, after that ye have suffered a while, make you perfect, stablish, strengthen, settle you." This is the part where a lot of Christians don't make it. Even though Jesus died for us to have a good life, there is going to be persecution. The devil is not going to just let you have what Christ died for you to have (the violent take it by force).

In 1 Peter 4:12-14, it says, "Beloved, think it not strange concerning the fiery trail which is to try you, as though some strange thing happened unto you: But rejoice, inasmuch as ye are partakers of Christ's sufferings; that, when his glory shall be revealed, ye may be glad also with exceeding joy. If ye be reproached for the name of Christ, happy are ye; for the spirit of glory and of God resteth upon you: on their part he is evil spoken of, but on your part he is glorified." It is not a surprise that we are going to go through some difficult things. Think about what Jesus went through, and they ended up killing him. But take heart! Jesus did it all for us. He put the devil where he belongs: under our feet. Keep him there. Do not let Jesus's death be in vain.

CHAPTER 10

—∿◠◠—

How to Receive What
Jesus Died for You to Have

Joshua 1:8 says, "This Book of the Law shall not depart out of your mouth, but you shall meditate in it day and night, that you may observe to do according to all that is written in it. For then you will make you way prosperous, and then you will have good success." With so many things to grab our attention and steal our time, Joshua 1:8 is the key to our very lives. God told Joshua that this book of the law should not depart out of his mouth, but that he should meditate on the word day and night, and the result would be that he would be prosperous and wise and have good success. It is kind of difficult to meditate on the word (which means to think deeply about it) and at the same time to worry about the negative things the devil tells us. Most people do not receive from God, because the devil feeds them lies. For example, if God says, "I will meet your need according to my riches in glory by Christ Jesus," and on the other hand the devil is whispering in your ear that you are not going to receive what God has promised you, you have a decision to make. Who are you going to believe, God or the devil? The devil works hard to get you to believe that the word will not work for you. Deception is all he has working for him. He has to get you to believe in his deception so he can get your confession of faith. Once you have moved out of faith and into unbelief, God can no longer do anything for you. Hebrews 11:6 says, "But without faith it is impossible to please him: for he that cometh to God must believe that he is, and that he is a rewarder of them that diligently seek him." Satan knows that God has great plans for us and that he cannot stop the blessing of God from coming to pass in our lives, but he can delay our blessing by getting us to doubt God's word. John 10:10 tells us what the devil has planned for us: "The thief cometh not, but for to steal, and to kill, and to destroy. I am come that they might have life, and that they might have it more abundantly." According to this scripture, it is obvious what the devil's intentions are concerning us. Jesus stripped the devil of all his power and gave it to us. The devil is defeated. He has no power, so he tries to trick people into believing that he has power that he does not. He only has deception working for him, so he deceives people and gets them to fear. Once you are in fear, you no longer are moving in faith. That is what the devil is counting on, because if he can get you out of faith and into fear, then what you are believing God for will never come to pass, and he will have you in doubt and unbelief. That is where he wants to keep you so he can continue to steal, kill, and destroy. He is trying to keep you from the abundant life that Jesus died for you to have. Jesus did not come to this earth and die a horrible death just so we could go to heaven one day. Let's go back to John 10:10. The second part of that verse says Jesus came so we could have life more abundantly. When you think of something being abundant, what comes to your mind? Do you think of more than enough, of overflow? I know that is just what Jesus came to give us. Jeremiah 29:11 is a really good scripture; it shows us what God has in store for us: "I know the plans I have for you, plans not to harm you but to give you hope and a future." We can see from this scripture that God has good things in store for us, but the devil comes to steal, kill, and destroy. God and Jesus come to ensure that we will have a good life. In 1 John 3:8, it says, "He that committeth sin is of the devil; for the devil sinneth from the beginning. For this purpose the Son of God was manifested, that he might destroy the works of the devil." As I said earlier, the devil has already been defeated by our Lord, Jesus Christ. He knows he has no authority over the born-again child of God, but if you do not know that, he will deceive you and try to make you think that he has all power. Really, he has none. Jesus wants us to take our place here on the earth and stop letting the devil run over us. He has no power but what we give him. God wants his people to prosper and be in health, as it says 3 John 1:2: "Beloved, I wish above all things that thou mayest prosper and be in health, even as thy soul prospereth." God wants the best for us, but it is up to us whether we receive everything that Jesus died for us to have. Deuteronomy 30:19 says, "I have set before you life and death, blessing and cursing: therefore choose life, that both thou and thy seed may live." Even though God wants the best for us, he has given us a choice, and we have to choose. He did not make us robots. In John 15:7, Jesus says, "If ye abide in me, and my word abide in you, ye shall ask what ye will, and it shall be done unto you." God's word in you is the key to answered prayer. Our Father wants us to be victorious in this life and enjoy all the rights and privileges that Jesus died for us to have. He desires that you keep his word, because it will keep you whole in spirit, soul, and body. John 8:32 says, "And you shall know the truth, and the truth shall make you free." The truth makes you free! It does not put you in bondage. To receive from God, you must be in agreement with what God says belongs to you. We are the determining factor in receiving from God. God's word does not change. God's will does not change. If you want to receive from God, you must change your believing and saying to agree with him. We receive by faith. Faith is believing what God says in his word regardless of what you see with your natural eyes or hear with your ears or feel with your senses. Faith believes God's word no matter what the circumstances say. Hebrews 11:1 says that faith is perceiving as real fact what is not yet revealed to the senses. When you receive or reject what God says in his word concerning you, you are dealing with his integrity. The Bible says that God is not a man that he should lie (Numbers 23:19). So if God says he wishes above all things that you should prosper and be in health as your soul prospers, that is what he means. Jesus came to deliver us from the curse of poverty, lack, and all the curses of the law. Galatians 3:13 says, "Christ has redeemed us from the curse of the law, having become a curse for us (for it is written, 'Cursed is everyone who hangs on a tree')." Sometimes you hear people say, "Well, I am waiting on God," but that is not correct, because God has already done what he is going to do. He sent his son to die so you could have life and that more abundantly. God has already done what he is going to do. The next move is on you. Do not let what Jesus did be in vain. He wants you to enjoy life to the full, so please do not take that for granted. Live the life Christ died for you to have. It is true that Jesus came to wash away sins, but he also came to destroy the works of the devil. He wants people to be healed and made whole, and we can only have that by destroying the power of the devil over our lives. When Jesus went to the cross, he stripped Satan of all the authority he had, and then he gave it to us to put the devil where he belongs: under our feet. Satan has no authority over you any longer if you are a born-again child of God. Colossians 1:13 says, "He [Jesus] has delivered us from the power of darkness and conveyed us into the kingdom of the Son of His love." But it is a personal matter what we will do with the authority that Jesus has given to us. Will we let Jesus's death be in vain and not receive what he has done to set us free from the devil? Or will you do as I have done and decide that you will have everything Jesus died for you to have? I am determined that I will have my peace, joy, prosperity, health, and everything else Jesus died for me to have (praise God).

John 3:16 says, "For God so loved the world that he gave his only son, that whoever believes in him should not perish but have eternal life." Well, I have made my mind up that I am *whoever* in that verse. Jesus did it all, but it is up to us whether we receive what Jesus did for us. I am like Joshua: as for me and my house, we shall serve the Lord. (Praise God.) As I said earlier, Jesus stripped the devil of all his power and authority and gave it to you and me. We have a choice to make: Will we use the authority given to us by Christ, or we will continue to let the devil rule over our lives? Jesus came to earth and died to ensure that we could overcome the devil. First John 3:8 says the son of God was manifested to destroy the works of the devil. I do not know about you, but to me that is great news. No longer do I have to let the devil lead me around and do what he wants. Remember, he comes only to steal, kill, and destroy. But the rest of that verse (John 10:10) says that Jesus came to give us life and that more abundantly. Praise God for Jesus. But if you go after the abundant life that Jesus died for you to have, do not think that the devil will sit still while you receive what Jesus died for you to have. But that's all right, because 1 John 4:4 says, "Greater is he who is in you than he who is in the world." Remember that the devil is defeated. He has no power. He only wants you to think that he does; that is how he rules over your life. But you do not have to let him continue to rule over you and manipulate your cares. Ephesians 6:10-13 says, "Finally, my brethren, be strong in the Lord and in the power of His might. Put on the whole amour of God, that you may be able to stand against the wiles of the devil. For we do not wrestle against flesh and blood, but against principalities, against powers, against the rulers of the darkness of this age, against spiritual hosts of wickedness in the heavenly places. Therefore take up the whole armour of God, that you may be able to withstand in the evil day, and having done all, to stand." I want to talk about the last phrase in that passage: "having done all, to stand." That is the key. We can outlast the devil in the name of Jesus. When you are standing on one of God's promises, you must first make a quality decision that you will keep your faith and apply it until you have the promise manifested in your life. You cannot succeed by trying to receive by faith. Commit yourself and all that you are without reservation to the fact that God's word is true no matter what you feel, see, or hear or what circumstances say. Say this out loud: "God's word does not fail. God's word shall come to pass in my life. I will not faint and lose courage. I will do all to stand, and therefore I will stand. I am like a tree planted by the waters. I shall not be moved by circumstances, people, or the devil. I stand on God's word. I will succeed and not fail. I will win and not lose."

After you have prayed the will of God, and have said with your mouth what you desire, and have believed that you have received, be ready to exert the force of patience until your faith produces the answer in the visible world. Hebrews 10:36 says, "For ye have need of patience, that after ye have done the will of God, ye might receive the promise." Do you notice that that verse says you *might* receive the promise? It is up to you. Along with our faith, we must have patience. Patience undergirds faith and keeps faith applied to whatever we are believing for until the result is manifested. When you learn to release the power of patience, you can receive anything from God that agrees with his word. When the devil tells you that God's word is not working in your life, patience rejects it as a lie. Patience has no fear. Patience knows that God's word has never failed in thousands of years. Patience knows that when faith is exercised to receive God's word, success is inevitable. Patience knows that the pit of corruption is already dug for the wicked. The devil is trying to get you to jump into the pit that has already been dug for him. Do not do it. Stand your ground on the word of God. The devil attacks every believer who attempts to live by faith; that is his job. But our job is to believe God and stand on his word no matter what. That is the only way God's promises will come to pass in our lives. The devil knows that. That is why he works so hard to try to stop us from believing God's word. Jesus died so you could have life and have it more abundantly, and as I said, the devil will try to stop you, but do not let him. Always remember that greater is he that is in you than he that is in the world. God loves you, and he wants his people to have abundant life here on this earth. Do not be intimidated by the devil. He is all huff and puff. "Be sober, be vigilant; because your adversary the devil, as a roaring lion, walketh about, seeking whom he may devour" (1 Peter 5:8). Note that the devil walks around *as* a roaring lion. It does not say he is one. Remember that Jesus stripped him of all his power. He has none; he only wants you to believe he has. He tries to get you to fear, but 2 Timothy 1:7 says, "For God hath not given us the spirit of fear; but of power, and of love, and of a sound mind." Rebuke that spirit of fear in the name of Jesus and tell the devil that God has not given you a spirit of fear. We must stand up to the devil. (I cannot say that enough.) That is the only way we will ever receive anything from God. But there is something else that can stop us from receiving from God. Be careful of the words you speak. Did you know that our angels can work for us to bring the blessing of God to pass in our lives? Hebrews 1:14 says, "Are they not all ministering spirits, sent forth to minister for them who shall be heirs of salvation?" The word *salvation* means "deliverance." We can put the angels to work on our behalf if we speak the words of God. Of course, if we do not speak the word, they cannot do anything for us; they hearken to the voice of God. Psalm 103:20 says, "Bless the Lord, ye his angels, that excel in strength, that do his commandments, hearkening unto the voice of his word." It is very important what you speak. The Bible says we are snared by the words of our mouths. With our words we can put our angels to work on our behalf, or we can curse our lives with our mouths. Our angels are waiting on our words. They cannot work against our words, and they will not work with our words. Notice what the angel tells Daniel in Daniel 10:12: "Then he said unto me, Fear not, Daniel; for from the first day that thou didst set thine heart to understand, and to chasten thyself before thy God, thy words were heard, and I am come for thy words." Words are important. They work for you or against you. The key to receiving the desires of your heart is to make the words of your mouth agree with what you want. Do not speak words that you do not want to come to pass. You can change your words from negative to positive as quickly as you can from positive to negative. Just take authority over words you have spoken that defeat your faith. If you have spoken words of doubt and fear, you can quickly amend them. Render those words powerless to come to pass. Negate them in the name of Jesus and reinstate what you want to come to pass. Your words either put the angels to work or force them to step back, bow their heads, and fold their hands. Your angels are waiting for you to give them words to bring to pass. They have been sent forth to minister for you. Give your angels something to do. Put them to work on your behalf by speaking what you want to come to pass according to the word of God. If the words you speak are not what you want to come to pass in your life, then do not speak them, because the key to receiving the desires of your heart is to make the words of your mouth agree with what you want to come to pass in your life. Our angels are waiting on us to give them something to do. I do not know about you, but I am keeping my angels busy working to bring to pass in my life what God has promised me. The devil works hard to get us to speak doubt and unbelief. He also knows that we have what we say. That is why it is so important to keep speaking God's word only. Let words of faith come out of your mouth, and then your angels can bring to pass what you say. The moment you exercise faith in your covenant, the angels go to work. There may be no evidence in the natural world that you are one step close to receiving your answer even one minute before it is manifested, so keep faithful words coming out of your mouth, because we have what we say.

CHAPTER 11

GOD HAS A PEOPLE ON THE EARTH (ARE YOU ONE OF THEM?)

"For the eyes of the Lord run to and fro throughout the whole earth, to shew himself strong in the behalf of them whose heart is perfect toward him" (2 Chronicles 16:9). God is looking to bless his people. That is why Jesus came—so we could have life in abundance. But God has had a problem getting his people to receive what Jesus died for us to have. When Jesus died on the cross and said, "It is finished," he meant we no longer have to live under the curse with sickness, poverty, depression, and all the other things the curse entailed. John 10:10 says that the devil comes to steal and kill and destroy, but Jesus came so we could have life and that more abundantly. Because of what Jesus did, we no longer have to live under the curse. By accepting Jesus into our lives, we are free from the curse, and we can live the abundant life that Jesus died for us to have. That is the reason he came. At one time we had no need for a savior, but when Adam and Eve sinned, the whole world was cursed, and we had need for a savior. Genesis 3:17 says, "Then to Adam He said, 'Because you have heeded the voice of your wife, and have eaten from the tree of which I commanded you, saying,

"You shall not eat of it": cursed is the ground for your sake; In toil you shall eat of it all the days of your life. Both thorns and thistles it shall bring forth for you, and you shall eat the herb of the field.'" Even though the world was cursed because of Adam and Eve's sin, God still made a way. He sent his only begotten son so that we might have life. Galatians 3:13 says, "Christ has redeemed us from the curse of the law, having become a curse for us (for it is written, 'Cursed is everyone who hangs on a tree')." We have been redeemed, set free from the curse of the law. Not only have we been redeemed from the curse, but it goes on to say in verse 14 that this redemption took place so that "the blessing of Abraham might come upon the Gentiles in Christ Jesus, that we might receive the promise of the Spirit through faith." God also wants us to receive the blessing of Abraham and live by faith. "Beloved, I pray that you may prosper in all things and be in health, just as your soul prospers, so God wants us to live in health and prosper in all things" (3 John 2). Psalm 35:27 says, "Let them shout for joy and be glad, who favor my righteous cause; and let them say continually, 'Let the Lord be magnified, who has pleasure in the prosperity of his servants.'" God also wants you to have prosperity in this life. Some people might frown at that statement, because religion has taught people that we are not supposed to have anything until we die and go to heaven. But I have news for you. We do not need prosperity when we get to heaven. We need it now while we are here on this earth. God wants us to live a good life. He wants us to have good health, sufficient finances, peace, joy, and all the other blessings Jesus died for us to receive, but only those who receive Christ in their lives will enjoy these blessings. John 3:16-17 says, "For God so loved the world that he gave his only begotten son, that whosoever believeth in him should not perish but have everlasting life. For God did not send His Son into the world to condemn the world, but that the world through Him might be saved." But just because God wants you to be blessed in this life does not mean you will be. You have an enemy, the devil, and he is trying hard to stop you from receiving what Jesus died for you to have. You have to put up a hard fight for what belongs to you in Christ. Isaiah 1:19 says, "If you are willing and obedient, you will eat the good of the land." The word *willing* is an action word. You must be determined that you will receive everything Jesus died for you to have. The scriptures show that God wants us to prosper, but the devil wants to keep us in poverty and lack. He knows that once we believe God's work and act on it, his days are numbered, so it is his job to try to keep us in bondage. He is terrified that we will believe the word of God and act on it, and then his days will be over in our lives. The devil is a defeated foe. He knows that, but the problem is that many people do not. Even some Christians don't know it, and that is what the devil has working for him. First of all, he tries to stop you from getting knowledge of the word, and if he cannot stop you from getting knowledge of the word, he goes to the next step, which is to stop you from acting on the word. James 2:14-17 says, "What does it profit, my brethren, if someone says he has faith but does not have works? Can faith save him? If a brother or sister is naked and destitute of daily food, and one of you says to them, 'Depart in peace, be warmed and filled,' but you do not give them the things which are needed for the body, what does it profit? Thus also faith by itself, if it does not have works, is dead." If we just have faith in God's word, that is not enough. For example, imagine you say you have faith that God will heal you and start out by standing on the word that by the stripes of Jesus you are healed. Then the symptoms get worse, and after a while you come away from the word. You begin to look at the circumstances, which are screaming a lot louder than what the word is saying, so finally you agree with your circumstances and say, "I am sick." It is a lot easier to believe what the circumstances are saying than to believe God's word. That is why it is so important to do what Joshua 1:8 says: "This book of the law shall not depart from your mouth, but you shall meditate in it day and night, that you may observe to do according to all that is written in it. For then you will make your way prosperous, and then you will have good success." According to this scripture, the only way we can look to the word is to meditate on it day and night. (To meditate means to think deeply about something.) That verse goes on to say that if you do that, you will make your way prosperous, and that is what God wants for you. He wants you to live a prosperous life and have good success. So not only do we have to meditate on the word, but we also have to have our minds renewed by the word of God. Romans 12:2 says, "And do not be conformed to this world, but be transformed by the renewing of your mind, that you may prove what is that good and acceptable and perfect will of God."

If we meditate on what the word says, we will not be fearful, confused, and living in unbelief. Our minds have to be renewed by the word of God. By meditating on the word, we prove what is the good and acceptable and perfect will of God for our lives. We have an enemy out there who is trying to keep us from the things of God, but 1 John 4:4 is a very encouraging scripture for us: "You are of God, little children, and have overcome them, because He who is in you is greater than he who is in the world." It does not matter what the devil is trying to do in your life; God is greater, and if you look to God, you cannot be defeated. The victory is already ours. We only have to stand in that victory. I am so thankful that I am a child of God and I know who I am in Christ. The devil tries hard to keep people from reading the word of God. As long as we do not know what the word says about a situation, we will continue to live a certain way. If you do not know that God wants you to be prosperous, then you will just keep living the way you are. And God wants to be able to bless you. Psalm 35:27 says, "Let them shout for joy and be glad, who favor my righteous cause; and let them say continually, 'Let the Lord be magnified, who has pleasure in the prosperity of his servant.'" You can see from this scripture that it gives God pleasure when his servants prosper. You might think, *Well, if God wants me to be prosperous, why doesn't he just make me prosperous?* It is true that God wants us to be prosperous, but we have something to say about whether we will have prosperity or not. Isaiah 1:19 says, "If you are willing and obedient, you shall eat the good of the land." The word *willing* in that verse is an action word. For example, imagine your employer says to you concerning your job, "Are you willing to work on weekends if needed?" If you tell your employer yes, then you have made a decision that if needed you will work on the weekends. We must do the same thing spiritually. We know that God wants us to prosper and eat the good of the land, so we need to make a decision that we will be prosperous and eat the good of the land. We see from God's word that he wants us to prosper, and we have made a decision that we will be prosperous. But there is someone on the earth who does not want you to prosper, and his name is Satan. John 10:10 says,

"The thief the devil does not come except to steal, and to kill, and to destroy. I have come that they may have life, and that they may have it more abundantly." I have decided in my personal life that I am going to have everything that Jesus died for me to have. I understand that the devil will try to stop me, but John 4:4 says that he who is in me is greater than he who is in the world. I don't just quote that scripture anymore; I know I have the revelation of that scripture. God in me is greater than all the demons in hell. God and I make an unbeatable pair. God needs us to take our rightful place here on the earth. The devil has been stealing and destroying in our lives long enough. We must stand up and let the forces of darkness know that enough is enough. God is on our side. Who can be against us?

God has given us dominion here on the earth. That means that the devil no longer has authority over us, and it is time that the body of Christ stood up to the devil. He is a defeated foe, and he can do only what we let him. I do not know about you, but I refuse to let the devil run my life another day. I am one of the people who is going to stand up and take my rightful place on this earth. There is a dying world out there, and they need our faith to get delivered from the devil. Ephesians 2:1-2 says, "And you He made alive, who were dead in trespasses and sins, in which you once walked according to the course of this world, according to the prince of the power of the air, the spirit who now works in the sons of disobedience." At one time we were in bondage to this world, but when we received Jesus into our hearts, the Bible says in Colossians 1:13 that we were delivered out of the kingdom of darkness into the kingdom of his dear son. (Praise God.) We are in another kingdom. The devil has no power over us anymore except what we let him have. So rise up in Jesus's name and put the devil where he belongs: under your feet.

Everything God promised you in his word belongs to you, but it is up to you whether you receive what God has provided for you in his word. I did not know that for many years, even after I was saved. I thought God would just provide us with whatever he promised us in his word and we just had to sit back and wait for it. But that is not the way it works at all. Isaiah 1:19 says, "If you are willing and obedient, you will eat the good of the land." The word *willing* here means "to be determined," and personally I am determined to receive everything God promised me in his word that belongs to me. When I found out that Jesus took our sickness in his body on the tree when he died for us settled it for me. When sickness tries to come on me, I rebuke it and tell it to get out of my body. I refuse to take it. Jesus already took my sickness. Why should I take it again? I do not deny the pain; I just deny its right to stay in my body. My body is blessed and not cursed. The Bible says in Galatians 3:13, "Christ hath redeemed us from the curse of the law, being made a curse for us: for it is written, cursed is every one that hangeth on a tree." and if that is not enough, 1 Peter 2:24 says Jesus "Himself bore our sins in His own body on the tree, that we, having died to sins, might live for righteousness—by whose stripes you were healed." The word works, but we have to work the word. Whatever the devil tries to put on you, you must come back with the word of God and refuse everything that he is trying to put on you. Most people, the saints included, think that Jesus died just so we would be saved and one day go to heaven. He did, but he also did a lot more than that. For one thing, salvation includes more than just a ticket to heaven when we die. John 10:10 says, "The thief cometh not, but to steal, and to kill, and to destroy; I am come that they might have life, and that they might have it more abundantly." Another scripture that shows how God wants us to have life here on the earth is Psalm 23. Verse 1 says, "The Lord is my shepherd; I shall not want," and verse 5 says, "thou preparest a table before me in the presence of mine enemies; thou anointest my head with oil, my cup runneth over." That has to be speaking about here on the earth, because in heaven there will be no enemies. Jesus wants us to have a wonderful life right here and now. That is the reason he came to this earth and gave his life as a sacrifice—so we could live the abundant life. But the devil is going to try everything he can to stop us from having the abundant life Jesus died for us to have, and one of the things the devil uses is fear. It says in 2 Timothy 1:7, "For God hath not given us the spirit of fear, but of power, and of love, and of a sound mind." The devil will always try to get you to fear. For example, say your rent is due and you are believing God that the money will come in and you will be able to pay your rent. You use the word on the devil and tell him that Philippians 4:19

says, "But my God shall supply all you need according to his riches in glory by Christ Jesus." You tell him the money will come in and your rent will be paid, and then you tell him to get out of your life in Jesus's name.

That is how you handle the devil—quote the scripture just as Jesus did. Jesus did not mess around with the devil. In Matthew 4:3-10, every time the devil tempted Jesus, he always came back with a scripture. But we have been letting the devil defeat us. He speaks negative things to our minds, and instead of coming back with the scriptures, we think about what he is saying and then begin to experience fear, doubt, and unbelief, and that is how the devil defeats us. But I have made up my mind that I am going to do what Jesus did and come back with what the word says. The devil is defeated. He knows it, but the problem is that a lot of the saints do not know it, because if they did, there would not be so much depression and powerlessness in the body of Christ. That is why it is important to know who you are in Christ and to know your covenant rights. You have a right to have joy. You have a right to divine healing. You have a right to live in prosperity. But just because you have the right does not mean that you will live that way; you must make a decision. Jesus died so we would live the abundant life, so I have decided that I will. But it is easier said than done unless you do what the word says in John 15:7: "If ye abide in me, and my words abide in you, ye shall ask what ye will, and it shall be done unto you." The word *abide* means to stay or set up a tent in a particular place. You won't be leaving—you are going to abide there. Too many of the saints do not really abide. Too many of us praise God on Sunday and forget about him until next Sunday. That is why the saints are living such defeated lives. If you do not give your physical body the food and water it needs, you will get weak, tire easily, and get sick. It is the same way with your spirit. If you neglect it and do not give it spiritual food, which is the word of God, it will get weak, and you will have no strength and will die spiritually. The devil will have a field day with you. Notice what Jesus says about that in Matthew 4:4: "Man shall not live by bread alone, but by every word that proceedeth out of the mouth of God." I cannot express how important it is for us to stay in the word of God. God told Joshua in Joshua 1:8, "This book of the law shall not depart from your mouth; you shall meditate on it in day and night, that you may observe to do according to all that is written in it. For then you will make your way prosperous, and then you will have good success." Reading and meditating in the word is the only way we can live the victorious life that Jesus gave his life for us to live. That is one thing the devil is afraid of. He knows that when we learn the will of God for our lives, we will put him under our feet where he belongs. Hosea 2:6 talks about how God's people perish for a lack of knowledge. The more you know, the more you are able to please God and the less hold the devil has on your life. In Numbers 13:1-2 when Moses sent the twelve spies to Canaan to spy out the land, God had promised the Israelites the land. The problem was that they did not think they could take the land as God said they could. Here is the report they give in Numbers 13:33: "There we saw the giants (the descendents of Anak came from the giants); and we were like grasshoppers in our own sight, and so we were in their sight." They said they were like grasshoppers, and that is why they could not take the land even though God said they could. It is all in how you see God in you. But two of the spies had a different spirit.

I am taking back what belongs to me. If the saints do not get a spirit like Joshua and Caleb, we will never receive anything that God has promised us, and that is what the devil is counting on. That is why he keeps us in doubt, unbelief, and especially fear. Why especially fear? Because fear paralyzes a person. It is like you are frozen and you cannot do anything. Remember that God has not given you a spirit of fear (1 Timothy 1:7). Until you make a decision that you are going to receive the inheritance that Jesus died for you to have, you will never live the abundant life that belongs to you. Deuteronomy 30:19 says, "I call heaven and earth as witness today against you, that I have set before you life and death, blessing and cursing; therefore choose life, that both you and your descendants may live. I call heaven and earth to record this day against you, that I have set before you life and death, blessing and cursing; therefore choose life, that both thou and thy seed may live." This is not only about us. The rest of the verse says "both you and your seed," so it is important that we get a revelation of the word not only for us but for our families and loved ones as well.

CHAPTER 12

The Key to Keeping Your Faith Strong in God

The number-one thing we must do to keep our faith strong in God is in Joshua 1:8: "This Book of the Law shall not depart from your mouth, but you shall meditate in it day and night, that you may observe to do according to all that is written in it. For then you will make your way prosperous, and then you will have good success."

I have found in my personal life that doing what God told Joshua to do, which is to read his word and meditate on his sayings at all times, will make you prosperous and cause you to have good success in life.

As saints of God, we must realize that we are in a fight for our lives. It's not a physical fight but a spiritual fight, notice what Ephesians 6:10 says about that: "For we do not wrestle against flesh and blood, but against principalities, against powers, against the rulers of the darkness of the age, against spiritual hosts of wickedness in the heavenly places." This scripture shows us that we are not up against people we can see but wicked spirits and unseen forces in the heavenly places. But verses 13 and 17 explain how we can handle that with God's word: "Therefore take up the whole armor of God, that you may be able to withstand in the evil day, and having done all, to stand . . . Stand, therefore, having girded your waist with truth, having put on the breastplate of righteousness, and having shod your feet with preparation of the gospel of peace; above all, taking the shield of faith with which you will be able to quench the fiery darts of the wicked one, and take the helmet of Salvation, and the sword of the Spirit, which is the word of God."

The main hindrance to increasing our faith in God's word is the spirit of fear. Notice what God's word has to say about fear in 2 Timothy 1:7: "For God has not given us a spirit of fear, but of power, and of love, and of a sound mind." God has given us many promises in his word, but the spirit of fear speaks to our minds and contradicts what God says. Take, for example, Philippians 4:13, where God says he will meet our needs according to his riches in glory by Christ Jesus. The spirit of fear tells you that God is not going to meet your needs; if he was, you would not be having such a hard time. The devil tells also you that God does not really care about you, because if he did, he would not let you suffer through this. But saints, we cannot listen to the lies of the devil. If God made a promise to you, you can believe that whatever he said will come to pass. On a personal note, I believe whatever God says, and it does not matter to me what circumstances look like. When it comes down to it, either you will believe God, or you will believe the lies of the devil. A scripture that encourages me can be found in John 16:33, where Jesus is speaking to his disciples and tells them that in the world they will have tribulation, but to be of good cheer, for he has overcome the world. Jesus is letting us know that there will be problems in this world, but he also says that he has overcome the world; and when Jesus overcame the world, he gave us the power to do the same.

"For whatever is born of God overcomes the world. And this is the victory that has overcome the world—our faith" (1 John 5:4). The scripture is saying that if we are born-again children of God, we can overcome the world with our faith in God. The devil is already defeated, and he knows it. But if he can mess with our minds and contradict what God says in his word and get us to believe it, he will destroy our faith in God. And the only way the devil can destroy our faith in God is to get us to listen to his lies that say the opposite of what God promises us. When you have real, biblical faith, you are not moved by what you see or hear. When circumstances are contrary to what the word of God says, you are not moved. Paul writes in 1 Corinthians 15:57, "Therefore, my beloved brethren, be ye steadfast, unmoveable, always abounding in the work of the Lord, forasmuch as ye know that your labour is not in vain in the Lord."

Something else of great importance in keeping our faith in God strong is praying in the Holy Ghost. Jude 1 verses 20-21 says, "But ye, beloved, building up yourselves on your most holy faith, praying in the Holy Ghost, Keep yourselves in the love of God, looking for the mercy of our Lord Jesus Christ unto eternal life." When we pray in the Holy Ghost, our spirit prays the perfect will of God for our situation. Romans 8:26-27 says, "Likewise the Spirit also helps in our weaknesses, For we do not know what we should pray for as we ought, but the Spirit Himself makes intercession for us with groaning which cannot be uttered. Now He who searches the hearts knows what the mind of the Spirit is, because He makes intercession for the saints according to the will of God." Sometimes we may not know exactly how to pray about a situation. When we pray in the spirit, we are praying the perfect will of God. Personally, I would rather pray in the spirit than in my natural tongue. I have noticed that things seem to happen sooner when I pray in the spirit concerning something.